Dear Soul:

Love after Pain

Sylvester McNutt III

D1059497

ISBN: 1511895640
ISBN-13: 978-1511895644

Connect with my personal website and social media sites listed below:

Instagram @sylvestermcnutt

Twitter @sylvestermcnutt

Facebook—facebook.com/sylvestermcnuttiii

Snapchat/Periscope @sylvestermcnutt

www.sylvestermcnutt.com

DEAR SOUL: LOVE AFTER PAIN

Imagine the sun as it beats across your chest, standing parallel to the horizon as we take in new oxygen from the universe. *Dear Soul* is a release of energy; it's a trade with the universe. This journey is an exchange that involves the release of our old soul as nutrients permeate our new soul. I challenge you to stand up right now and make the same gesture that's pictured here. This book was created to inspire, uplift, and ignite your inner core. I challenge you to let go of any negative energy that is clouding your soul and enjoy this book of poetry.

2

SOUL

We live in a generation that lacks authenticity, honesty, and empathy. We do not understand each other or each other's struggles as human beings. Today, my culture needs more love and understanding than ever before. We need more healing, growing, and development than ever before.

Our souls are being killed by technology, expectation, and separation. *Dear Soul* is my attempt at laying the groundwork for recovery, healing, and moving forward. *Dear Soul* is my journey journal written in conversationalist tone, a very intimate, introspective style of poetry, and it shows the twisted romantic observations of the world, which we have all seen.

This book connects to every human because it is based on finding love after pain. Pain is something that is common to each of our stories. Let's be honest—how many of us are still suffering from incidents from our childhood? When we struggle in life, the problem is not the problem. The problem is not having adequate solutions or resources to really move forward from the stresses.

Dear Soul is the ultimate book to help you take an introspective look inside to uncover a deeper connection with self and a deeper scope for possible solutions for any type of pain.

As a writer, my style has been dubbed "visionary poetry," and my purpose is to combine observations, poetry, and persuasive logic. My only goal is to cause an intense amount of thought or reflection inside of each reader. I do not put my words together to be "right." Right and wrong are relative and based on a person's perception and experience. It would be egregious of you to tell me that anything I am writing about is wrong, and vice versa. Nothing is wrong; everything in life is all about perception and perspective. The user who will get the most from this book is one who will relate to the topics that are relevant to his or her personal growth. The other user is someone who will step outside of his or her bubble and understand another's struggle. Once you can holistically understand another person's struggle, then you have activated empathy, and I believe that empathy is the most important quality missing from our culture.

Once you have a culture of people who understand each other, are comfortable with self, and able to communicate effectively, then you raise the vibration of the entire world with that energy.

We sit inside of our bubbles and internalize the pain of everything that happens to us, but we don't align with our struggles or successes. I am genuinely happy when I see people succeed at something they've worked for. I am able to share the joy as if it were my own accomplishment. I am able to feel the pain of a woman who doesn't feel comfortable walking down the street at night alone. No, I have never been a woman, but I have listened to those stories and tried to put myself there. Let's just be honest. This generation does not talk about sex, race, or pain from our childhood.

We ignore those topics and we ignore self-love. I never heard the word *self-love* when I was growing up. As a child, I also didn't hear the word *love* much. I went on several spiritual journeys in my early twenties to discover the deepest version of self. What I present to you here is a continuation of the journey. I am happy, I am healed, and I am as healthy as I can be. Today, I am sharing a spiritual, emotional, and health journey with you inside of these lines.

Your Benefit for Reading *Dear Soul*

My goal with this project is to have the information presented just like how it would be in a personal journal. If you do not know much of my story, I will share something very important with you.

As a child I suffered from depression, anger, and suicidal thoughts. I was a victim of domestic abuse and grew up with alcoholic parents. I dealt with rejection, a massive heartbreak, and the constant impression of feeling unwanted as a product of abandonment. The past also produced unresolved grief, obsessive work ethic, and massive paranoia.

These are things that I dealt with and overcame as a product of training, learning, growing, healing, and writing. I turned to writing as a coping mechanism for what life presented me. *The Dear Queen Journey* and *Dear Soul* are both books to help instill more love. Today, I am in a very happy place, as I resolved the grief. I got over the ex and developed a high-level sense of self, which doesn't allow the paranoia to ruin me. I am not writing this book as a person who is trying to heal or grow from these steps. That wouldn't be fair for the reader. However, I do encourage you to write and dive deep into your own story. I guarantee that writing your story, from yourself to yourself, will change your life. I'm very grateful to be able to stand on this side of the pendulum, and I hope I can give my reader the same benefits.

As an artist I feel like the traditional book standards are very boring, and I feel like a lot of readers get lost in the abyss of big words and super long chapters. My goal here is to stay true to my personal writing format and myself. I enjoy the journal format. After reading this book over several times, I truly feel like it will impact every single person who reads it in a positive way.

The power that lies within me is within you. My soul recognizes your soul, and before we go any further, I need you to read this next section aloud.

Soul Affirmations

I Will Change the World

I Am the World

I Am Society

I Am Important

I Deserve Joy

I Deserve Abundance

My Soul Deserves to Vibrate Higher

There Is Nothing That I Cannot Do

I Am Special

I Will Overcome

The Power Is Already Inside of Me

I love seeing recovery and growth in my fellow humans. For a person to go from a situation of suffrage and oppression to joy and happiness is refreshing. Nobody has a perfect life, but we all have a worth-it life. No matter what, never forget that you can overcome any obstacle. You are the one. You are the most important person in this movie. Never forget that you have the ability to rewrite the script at any moment. The first step you need toward happiness, success, and love is vision. You have to see where you want to go; create a vision and die for it.

—Sylvester McNutt III ("**Vision**")

Happier people are oftentimes people who resonate with a dream, goal, or vision. The idea of a vision creates a mind-set of achievement. It creates, upon completion, the feeling of fulfillment and gratefulness. When vision is present, it becomes the backbone of a person's life, standing as the purpose. If you lack vision of what your purpose is, then looking at what gives you joy and happiness is most likely a part of your vision. The amazing thing about vision and its correlation with happiness is you do not always have to actually see how your vision will come true. You just have to know and believe that it exists. For example, imagine the first time you walked up the stairs. Something you may not remember, but it's something that happened after taking action toward the goal. You were so young that you probably don't even remember this event occurring the first time, and now you do it as second nature. You completed that vision because of two things:

- You took the first step to do it (literally).
- You believed in where you would end up.

Happiness itself is a vision. If you find yourself not as a happy as you would like to be, then I invite you to simply shift your mind around the idea that you are already happy. Regardless of your situation, I challenge you—one may think his or her situation is the worst and unrecoverable, but I guarantee you no matter what you are dealing with right now today, it could be much worse. Plus, when you push your mind to believe that you are already happy even with a lack of vision, or lack of desired situation, you will consciously create the situation you desire. Scientists have noted that smiling while in a bad mood will push your bad mood away. I encourage you to find your purpose, find the reason you do what you do, and apply your vision to it. Happy people allow their vision to guide them toward their happiness because it is a state of mind; it is a mind-set and a culture. Regarding vision and the execution of vision into your life to create the happiness and bliss you deserve, I invite you to do these two things:

1. Write your vision down in a place that you will see it every day.
2. Speak about your vision as often as possible to friends, family, and colleagues.

The Approval of Others

First of all, you do not need anyone's validation at all to exist and be happy. You are already excellent the way you are, and nobody needs to come in your life and tell you that. There are thousands of reasons that you should never seek the validation of others.

It's a time-consuming process, asking people what they think about you and why. Another reason is that you cannot control what people think. You do not have the power to control any other person besides yourself. You literally are the only person you can control, so you have to give up the desire to want to find out what people think about you.

You have the freedom to be whom you want, think what you want, and do what you want. So tell me, please tell me, why do you need another person to give you permission to do that? I agree that you should be open to other people and open to ideas. However, it is not your duty to live in a state of seeking validation.

You have to remember this crucial factor about approval addiction; it requires that someone provide you his or her opinion. An opinion is only a story or idea. It is not something that sits in facts or laws. I encourage you to run from stories—they are the equivalent of a fable or fairy tale. You would never live your life based off stories from the Disney movie *Lion King*. So why live off stories from random people who do not speak on facts? Base your life inside of logical analysis and an understanding of self. It's irresponsible for you to constantly seek others' approval. That means you're living by their compliments and dying by their negativity.

The point is this: You are your own best friend. You should think well of yourself and highly of yourself.

I wrote a poem a few years ago called, "Who Is She Pretending to Be?" The poem was focused around a girl who remained confused due to her addiction to seek approval of others and change who she was just so people could validate her. A friend who consistently wanted validation inspired the poem. I never understood why she was looking for people to justify her looks and her personality. I exclaimed to her, "You are fine just the way you are. Why do you keep changing yourself to fit other people's idea of what you should be?"

Here is what you should focus on:

- Find your vision and allow your vision to drive you.
- Remain open to other people's ideas and thoughts but always recognize that your own thoughts about yourself are the only ones that truly matter.
- Stop being so critical of yourself.

Wake up every day and realize three things. The first thing you should do is realize that you are already excellent. Everyone on this planet wants to improve and get better, but that does not mean that you are not already excellent. The second item you should bring into your consciousness is that no other human is a benchmark for your success or beauty. You are special and perfect just the way you are. Each of us has a different anatomy and spirit. The third thing you should do is recognize that nobody will ever be able to give you what you need and that everything you need comes from within. Your intrinsic value can only be justified by you.

Excuses

If you want to achieve any type of happiness, you have to understand that excuses are the poor man's way to unhappiness. Excuses are bridges, and they allow you to go to a place that is a place we like to call *nowhere*. Excuses build bridges to nowhere. Does that sound like an ideal destination?

Making excuses allows the user to become removed from the idea of responsibility and accountability. In other words, there can be no consequence or reaction for your actions or lack of actions. Excuses belittle the user in any situation and allow a person to be separate from his or her own personal power. The power that exists inside of every person gets turned up or down, based upon one's actions. I reassure you that making excuses only turns down your ability to gain and use your power. Making excuses puts you in a state of mind where your environment and circumstance will actually control you. It becomes a state of mind where "when it rains, it pours."

My invitation to you is a grand one, but it is one that will single handedly change your life in a way that has never occurred before. In order to stop making excuses, I invite you to do these two things:

- Assume everything that happens regardless the outcome was a direct result of your action/inactions.
- Realize that being accountable and responsible for your actions will allow you to improve them.

I see a world of very damaged and sick people, yet most of them do not even realize their deficiencies. This is largely due to the excuses people make and something called *social justification*. It's a legal term that applies to a situation where the public agrees to the outcome of a legal case. The majority of what your life is right now is a congruent conglomerate of outcomes. They are the results of actions of the last few years. The second you assume responsibility and stop making excuses is the second that you

11

change the life that you are currently living. Other people around you justify your life because they never call you out on anything and allow you to continue living the way you are. It never fails—100 percent of the time, persons who are able to understand their cognitions would like to improve on something. When given the opportunity to improve, what most do not understand is why they do not.

First, they have been conditioned and are used to a certain baseline of expected behavior. And second, there is usually nobody present to push them beyond that baseline. I urge you to take an examination of your life and see who allows you to live the way you live. Why are these people allowing you to make excuses?

Nobody is exempt from this. If you were supposed to get back in the gym, take that vacation, put more money in your emergency fund, et cetera—I know excuses exist, because people tell me every day about what they want to do and what they wish they were doing. My invitation is simple: stop making excuses, and start executing on what you want.

Everything in life revolves around the same few principles. If I say you need to try hard in your business to make more money, it will resonate with people who want to make more money. But if I say you need to try harder in your relationship to love each other deeper, it will trigger those who are looking for a deeper love. From an objective view, all principles in life are the same, and if you're a lazy person who makes excuses, you'll never reach any of your goals. I suppose you need luck with your excuses if that is you, so "good luck."

Gratitude

This is the feeling or attitude in acknowledgment of a benefit that one has received or will receive. Any religion that you may or may not participate in will have a pillar of gratitude involved in it. This is such a powerful emotion and such a positive one that psychology just started studying it, and when I say "just," I mean as recent as the year 2000. With most adults believing in some sort of higher power, whether it's a being that we call "God" or a belief in the "universe," there is something to pull from each group, and it is the damnedest thing if you look objectively. The practice of gratitude—it is the most powerful tool you have when it comes to happiness, as you are literally giving away power. You are empowering the people around you. I invite you to make these three phrases exist by calling these people right now:

- (Mom, dad, brother, sister) "I am glad that we are in the same family because of…"
- (Coworker, boss, employee, assistant) "I really appreciate the hard work you do because…"
- (Friend) You have been a great friend to me, and I want to thank you because…"

These phrases said with sincerity and real-life application will change your life. I guarantee it. If you don't believe me, try it right now and let's see what happens. People who practice being grateful have higher levels of control of their environments, personal growth, and purpose in life. People who practice and believe in being grateful accept themselves and their situations at a more efficient rate. Multiple studies and doctors have supported that gratitude is the father of all pillars of mental well-being.

In conclusion, I invite you to become a person who praises instead of who criticizes. I encourage you to become a person who sees why you are grateful of what you do have and one who does not hyperobsess about things you do not have. I hope you focus on being grateful for your situation and the people involved in your life. Take some of the practices that we provided here and let the people around you know their worth and how much you appreciate them.

Give

One of the most powerful tools you will ever have is your ability to give. Giving allows your mind to believe that you already have enough, and having enough is the equivalent of being fulfilled. A fulfilled person is a person who must be happy—this logically makes sense.

Studies show that people who volunteer their time or services heal better and live life at a happier sustained rate versus those who do not. There is a balancing act that occurs when you give; typically it revolves around the fact that you are taking less.

You can give in abundance, the same way you can take or desire to want at an abundant level. From a study conducted by Compassion.com, low-income families, who have less financial flexibility than middle- and upper-class families, donate 4.5 percent of their income, where the upper class donate 3 percent and the middle class 2.5 percent.

Giving is not just about material items and goods. It is mostly about things that possess intrinsic value, such as time, compassion, or listening. Individuals are different as far as what they have to offer from a giving perspective, but we all have something to give.

For some of us, our gift may be what enables us to give, or maybe it's just something we are passionate about. For me personally, writing is one of the only talents I have—it is one of the only talents I have that gets drilled over daily to improve it. I believe that I can give that to the world and help the world.

A friend of mine named Jeremy used to DJ at a bar and work a forty-hour-a-week job. He never complained about DJ-ing or dealing with drunken idiots. He was elated and ecstatic to go DJ every Sunday because he got joy out of it. His skill allowed him to control the party and to ensure that the patrons of his bar had a great time. More importantly, his passion for playing music allowed him to let go of his daily stresses and focus on something fun. He helped people and helped himself at the same time.

If you are currently living a life where giving is absent, I invite you give more and take less—and watch happiness take over your life.

No Cover-Up

There is no reason to run from the truth. There's no vendetta that needs to be repaid. Allow this second to be your moment of clarity, the moment of truth. Accountability is your friend. Being responsible for your participation in any toxicity that you've experienced is first. Today we will not cover up anything that others have done to us either. Just because they have a title doesn't mean their behavior is not subject to observation and accountability. No masks, nothing to hide—we can be, and we must be, naked. We have a craving for freedom, and we will be free because after today, we will not speak about ourselves like we are victims. We will not make excuses for others anymore; today is the day of recreation.

One of the most freeing feelings is to know that you've moved on from a toxic situation. When we are in the madness, we struggle to identify it.

However, once you see it and then take steps to improve your life, eventually you'll sigh in relief and happiness. An axiom of life is that nothing is forever, not even life. This fact should reinforce our ability to be grateful for what we have and to let go of toxic things that prevent us from a steady state of joy. It would be irresponsible of me to tell you what you deserve, so the question is, what do you deserve? Do you deserve happiness, freedom, and joy, or is it just a pipe dream?

The Fall

All persons go through struggles that leave them displaced, answerless, and full of questions.

It's up to users to recover from the grip of gravity as it slams them down into the depths of confusion.

The only thing you can do is wake up, pay attention, and have deeper conversations with yourself.

"The Fall" is an adverse action against your soul that plunges you into fear, illusion, or guardedness.

As you fall from that shaky ground that you used to stand on, and you find yourself plummeting into nothingness, don't worry about when it will stop.

There will be too much pressure if you're thinking about slaying all of these issues. Just start with one, and take it one day at a time.

The Jaded

There have been so many parts of life that have
stripped us of our innocent, naïve nature.

Then we become a jaded sphere of dejection
because it feels like nobody can comprehend.

You just sit inside of the abyss of nonexistence
feeling like all of the ordinances that have been
formed against you are winning.

The fall hits you like a ton of bricks, falling from
Venus right on top of the epicenter of your
mental earthquake.

The pain from the past forces you to become a
reflection of the empty souls who have ruined
your will. Now you're sitting on a throne of fear
and insecurity.

You become "The Jaded."

The Paradoxes

The paradoxes of life never gave me much — they only took and took, leaving me empty and cold like a hot plate that nobody wanted. My emotions, equivalent to the nutrition from the food, just sat at the table unwanted and unattended to. I always wanted someone to sit at my table and appreciate what I had to offer. I just wanted to know that I was good enough for consideration.

The paradox of not being wanted caused me to become toxic like my environments. It caused me to distance myself from people, even though we need people to feel inclusive. This is the clouded paradox that I'll never understand: how it's a basic human need to feel like we belong, but then the people who bring us into this earth do not want us. What a fucking paradox that is.

The toughest paradox to deal with is the one where you feel like you don't belong where you should. You want to be able to walk up to the other kids who look just like you in school, but instead they crack jokes. You want your parents and family unit to be solid and full of life, but it appears as if the broken family model is more dominant in this culture. This is a product of being broken as people and not recovering. If you ask me, it's a cycle of devastation. When people get hurt, they pass their insecurities and fears to their children. Those children then don't know self, so they destroy the people they date, and then they become a part of the jaded from the fall. It's a cycle of pain, and that is the paradox that I never understood.

Listening

Most people don't listen well. We have two ears, yet most people only know how to speak. Imagine what you could hear if you put effort and energy into listening as an actual skill. Most people who spend time speaking do not actually know what they're talking about, or how to go about getting their messages across in an effective way. Most people just speak and talk without any purpose or direction; it is just a bunch of words vomiting from their brain through their throat.

The ego wants to be heard, but there's more value in the silence and observation. The silence allows you to hear the darkness of everyone's thoughts. The darkness of each other's thoughts allows us to align, connect, and empathize. The way we heal and grow our communities is through active listening, which is the art of being concerned with what the other soul is speaking on. Waiting for your turn to speak is not conversation— it's dysfunctional communication. In the communication model, the sender's message is only efficient once the receiver actually receives and decodes the message. Listening also requires you to get off of your cell phone and to look people in the eye. Listening is about paraphrasing and repeating what they said, for understanding. This skill will change everything about your human experience.

Family Kill

The hardest thing to deal with as a child is parents who do not understand you. Parents who force you to be a particular way based on their childhood, or what they feel like a child should be like.

Let's just be honest—your family can kill your progress and happiness. Just because people are in the same family does not mean they have your back or that they're going to uphold the respect that should come with a title like "brother" or "mother."

I guess...

The key is to always remember that you cannot help the family you were born into, but you can help the family you create.

My Biggest Regrets

I wish I wouldn't have been so shy and scared to speak up when I was hurt or placed in a situation that made me uncomfortable. Looking back on my life, I realize I thought like a victim. I was looking at things and asking myself, "Why are these things happening to me?" I was a victim with a victim's mind-set. Thinking like that always kept me as a slave. If you're not obsessed with freedom, you'll never, ever achieve it. Fear controlled me. Even if the fear was not real, it was my perception at the time. I was terrified to speak up when people hurt me, when life was confusing.

To avoid regrets, try these three things:

1. *Never feel alone when you are going through a hard time*. Don't isolate yourself, because somewhere, there is a person who can help you through, but you also have to help you.

2. *Take action*. It's not okay to be a victim and to think like a victim. The most important mental trick is to stop thinking like a victim, which will cause you to require more of how you want to be treated.

3. *Speak up and don't hold in the frustration of feeling like you can't; do it tactfully*. When you're going through it, you just don't feel like it is feasible to speak up. Finding the right person and voicing your thoughts will always be crucial to your success.

I Promise

I never understood growing up like this. Why did our parents treat us like we had a choice to be here? I didn't ask to be on this planet, dammit. Why can't parents remember that they create children and evolve as people and leaders? I feel like my parents were directors in a Broadway show. I was one of their lead puppeteers; we were each other's audience as we destroyed each other on stage every night. One night my father told me to come into his room. He was drunk and wanted to teach me a lesson, so he pushed the clip into his black pistol and pointed it at my face. This was the very first time I felt my heart stop.

Picture yourself standing there frozen and cold like the tundra. Your eyes locked and fixated on the steel shaft. You notice a hand wrapped around the rubber grip. And the most eerie part of it all was seeing the eyes on the other end that looked just like mine. Do you know what it feels like to be trapped, to be a slave inside your own house? They make you feel like you're the antagonist to their happiness even though you're just a person who doesn't understand life. Do you know what it feels like to want to cry every day, but you've run out of tears and energy to cry?

This letter is not asking for pity or sorrow. It's a reflection of my past in order to gain perspective on a parental weakness that I dealt with. I promise not to allow myself to be abused. I promise not to abuse my wife or my children.

Better in the Dark

It was better when my parents left the room,

turned off the lights, and closed the door

behind them.

I didn't want to see the monsters.

Most kids are afraid of the monsters under the

bed.

I had real-life monsters; they were much more

vicious than victorious.

The main reason I liked the dark was because

I knew I didn't have to see them anymore, and

that is why my vision is perfect in the dark.

Child Touch

We have a serious problem in our culture that we cannot ignore anymore. According to VictimsofCrime.org, too many children are growing up with the common experience of sexual abuse. One in five girls and one in twenty boys are victims of child abuse. Three out of four adolescents who were victimized reported the oppressor to be a familiar face.

As a culture we mustn't run from having open conversations with each other about the company we keep. I have had very intimate conversations with my male friends about their consumption hours of pornography, about their sexual experiences, and about how they view women. I will not allow my daughter around people who do not respect the essence of protecting the purity of children. Honestly, you don't really know what any human is capable of, but I do feel like as a protector you can choose safe environments. There are warning signs, and there are ways to educate your child without instilling fear. This topic is very sensitive to us, and I hope you really take a look at whom you allow in your circle and in the presence of your children, if and when you have them.

How Dreams Feel

My dreams are appalling and lucid,
lungs collapsing and air escaping
even though I am aware of my consciousness.
Reality seems like life, a cynical fairy tale.

Born in the darkness, enjoying the tangled roots
of life as conflict wraps around my soul like a
river that meanders through
a South American country.

I can never run or jump, but I never die.
My dreams allow me to get so close to death that I become drawn to it like ants when
fruit falls to the cement. I love the abyss and free feeling of reaching out for someone to
grab me, but there's nobody around.

These dreams we have are movies, pictures of the moments we have throughout life.
Dreams can be visualizations for greatness, for sorrow or entertainment. My dreams are
so scary and real that I avoid sleep because I cannot tell the difference between this
fictional reality and that falsified fantasy that I am sold every day. It's all a blur now; my
soul doesn't recognize a difference. All I know is, my soul wants happiness.

Wicked Games

You're never going to win the wicked games,

the ones that life plays with us like we are the chords of a piano.

All you can do is allow life to push and tap you

when it feels like you deserve the vibration.

Just be ready to make harmony and justice with your

beautiful soul when it is called upon. You are not a sad song.

You are the moment a butterfly finally takes flights.

—Sylvester McNutt III

Five Behaviors to

Elite Mental Strength

1. Visualize things that do not currently exist.

2. Develop a routine that allows you to develop consistency.

3. Do not attach your worth to outcomes—only effort and behavior.

4. Stop comparing yourself to other people or old versions of yourself.

5. Listen to cleaner music. Subject yourself to less negativity from media.

There is peace

on the other side

of acceptance.

There is stress

in any other state.

—Sylvester McNutt III

Five Stages of Loss and Grief

One of the most important psychology books in our century was published in 1969, called *On Death and Dying* by Dr. Elizabeth Kübler-Ross. In this book she proposed a very famous idea about the five stages of loss and grief.

If you're familiar with this material, please bear with me. If you're new to the material, these are the five stages listed below.

The five stages of grief and loss are:

- denial and Isolation
- anger
- bargaining
- depression
- acceptance

I'd like to share a personal story that I recently went through that I think can really add value to other people's experience around this topic. I started dating a woman I had an instant connection with. We shared common ideologies on the world, spirituality, and life. We shared similar lifestyles and even had similar interests in music. On paper we were perfect for each other. We started hanging out, and it was amazing, at least on my end. I allowed my mind to develop those fantasies that we hopeless romantics allow to kill our sense of the now. I never felt so good about my initial spark with a person. It felt like magic. That's what's missing from love these days—magic. People have forgotten how to fall in love. I wanted to take that magic and morph it into something sustainable and respectful for both of our needs. I gave her all of my attention, I made her the screen saver on my phone, and I even told the women I was talking to previously that I no longer could talk to them because I wanted to focus on this one. Honestly, she was so gorgeous to me as a person inside and out. However, there were two things working against me that I wasn't really aware of. The first was that she met me at a vulnerable time in her life, and I suppose she wasn't "ready."

Now, I put ready in quotations because I write how I speak, and in person when I tell this story I do the little quotation fingers because I'm almost mocking the statement. In my last book, *The Dear Queen Journey: A Path to Self Love*, I talk about how there's no such things as "ready," and that blessings come and go, and that you should be ready to accept them. From my perspective, I just have a hard time "accepting" when people say they're not ready.

The second part of it was that she became mentally detached after the spark went down and it became a normal interaction. Once those two things mixed together, she withdrew from the situation. She stopped calling, she stopped coming over, and she stopped engaging in conversation like we once did. It hurt me bad. It hurt me really bad because I had so much hope in what we could've been. I took time off from dating to find myself after that. It was a rough situation; it's tough when there's a person who gives you everything just to pull back when the emotions get involved, well to say the least I became very hurt from this situation because I didn't want to accept it. I couldn't accept it because I invested time, I sacrificed, and I hoped for the future.

30

Here's the stages I went through:

- **Denial and Isolation**—I stopped talking to friends and family and couldn't believe when she told me, "I want to pull back because I am not ready." I was really frustrated because in my mind she already had the key to the house.

- **Anger**—I went on a rage, deleting all her pictures off my phone and even sending them to her and saying stuff like, "I'm deleting this picture. You can have it if you want it." Of course I did this because I was angry and didn't want to accept her decision.

- **Bargaining**—I called her and texted her to gain an understanding of "why." I wanted to know why, and the reason I wanted to know why is because it helps with closure. *Closure* is what relationship experts might call it, but I believe more important than closure is *acceptance*. The reason for that is because you may never get a *closure* meeting or conversation with a person—sometimes people die, and the only thing you have left is acceptance. You heal once you accept. But when you're in this bargaining stage, you get to your lowest point because you're willing to give up parts of your identity just to change another person's mind or outcome. That's not fair to you, ever. If you find yourself begging, pleading, and asking for something, you may be in this negotiation stage, and this stage can make you go delusional. Be aware of this.

- **Depression**—I didn't fall into depression, but many do, and depression is nothing to play with. It takes you through a wide variety of moods and swings that can last days and even hours if not paid attention to. Typically, you may resonate with feelings of anger or extreme sadness and withdrawal. Again, after a loss, this feeling is normal. But following that is the most important stage you want to land on. In my situation with this women, I avoided depression because I knew self, and there wasn't enough time invested in her to warrant such a violent mood swing. However, I became sad and angry, but it didn't turn into depression. If you find yourself in depression, I urge you to seek professional help, plus add positive actions to your day to day.

- **Acceptance** — I finally accepted her decision. I realized the reality was that she no longer wanted a relationship, and I gave up trying to change her mind about us. Instead, I focused on changing my mind about her. The best thing I did was live in a lane where my only option was to appreciate and accept her decision to move on without me. Yes, it hurt my ego at that very moment, but there is no progress with the ego, ever. I didn't begin to heal until I let go; letting go is rooted in acceptance.

Once I finally accepted her decision, I realized that she was the one who made a mistake and she was the one losing out. Ironically, I kind of look at it as dodging a bullet, because if a person doesn't see your worth and you fight and try to convince that individual that you're worthy, that's not pure self-motivated motivation. That's more like persuasion or trickery, and you shouldn't need to run a magic trick just to get a person to like you back. That's crazy as hell, actually. If you're just tricking or convincing people to be with you, then that just means you understand the art of seduction, and my goal is not to seduce a person into being with me. I don't think that should be yours either. I don't recommend solely seducing a person to like you. I've seen organic relationships develop when both people have the intrinsic motivation to work for and desire each other. Don't chase a person who doesn't want you—that's a plan of failure.

Do you like the constant heartbreak and heartache of trying to convince another person to see the value in you?

In conclusion, I bring this topic up because a lot of this book is rooted in the idea of acceptance. I find that acceptance is the golden ticket to success and happiness, and we are never going to get over these dark childhoods that we were handed unless we start understanding acceptance. If you want to move your life to the next phase, you have to move it away from denial and anger, and it has to go into acceptance.

The bridge of denial and anger leads us to nowhere. Your soul cannot and shouldn't force the compatibility of whichever region you may naturally be in. Always remember that each one of life's paths can go through the other in any order. Think about the all-star athlete in high school who then becomes a freshman in college and is now at the bottom of the depth chart trying to learn a new game. Think about the sales rep who is in the top 1 percent of sales in a company, and now after a promotion is a clueless manager and has to start all over.

You may jump back from acceptance to denial and into depression—this is very possible. However, the baseline that we must understand is that acceptance is the stage that offers the most peace, the most longevity, and the most progress. The other stages offer a multitude of solutions and positive growth, and they are indeed "normal." I don't want you to look at denial like you should avoid it. When someone breaks off a relationship, when someone dies, or when a person betrays, we often ask questions like,

"Why me and why now?" I remember when my father passed last year. I kept asking my consciousness one question and one question only, "Why?" Dealing with death is something that is natural. It's actually a part of life, and I encourage the souls reading this book to really grasp these concepts because they are required for mental health.

Everyone dies; therefore we typically all know someone who dies. The experience of death is something that is frowned upon and met with sad connotations. I'm honestly trying my best to understand why that is. I feel like we celebrate life and we mourn death. However, it doesn't really seem that natural to me. I feel like we should celebrate the life of the deceased. I honestly hate funerals, and it's normal for us to feel sad and cry. The truth for me is that I hate both of those emotions. I enjoy happiness much more.

I suppose I have no control over how my funeral will be, but I genuinely do not want some boring ceremony with a bunch of flowers. I don't like flowers, I don't like sad music, and I really don't like a bunch of sad people. *Dear Soul* can stand as my living will and testament. It's bigger than just a journal. I want my life to be remembered and celebrated for the good I have caused and the lives I have impacted. I do not want people crying and wearing black suits all night.

In conclusion, I want you to remember that your path is yours and that you do not have to flow through this process in any particular way. The speed of your healing, growing, or moving-on process is determined by your mental health, the level of attachment to the stimuli causing this pain, and most importantly your desire to reach acceptance.

We often force our mind away from acceptance because of our fantasies. That is why we stay stuck in jobs, relationships, and behaviors that keep us away from our potential. You move on from your ex. You get a better job and health when you develop a relationship with acceptance. Acceptance forces the user to live inside of reality—versus that obscure, distorted fantasy created in the mind.

Acceptance is the bridge to recovery, happiness, and success. It's the path that will move you forward when life jolts you with two steps backward. Just because you lose your placement doesn't mean you can't walk. Broken ankles, feet, and legs always heal, and never forget that.

Sometimes the people who are supposed to love you act like they hate you. The key is not to change them; your key to happiness is acceptance. Your key is to understand that love doesn't make you act that way. That's not love.

—Sylvester McNutt III ("Acceptance Was")

Tunnel Vision

There is an innate ability inside of each human to reach a higher level of consciousness than what they currently have. Your personal journey of awakening and growing is determined by your personal growth and desire. You do not have to grow at a pace that is not safe for you. You do not have to have another's expectation of how your growth journey should go. Always have vision for yourself. The biggest crime I see when it comes to personal development is people who do not have a plan or purpose for what they're doing. There is literally no purpose in maneuvering without knowing what you're doing. In contrast, the *Titanic* was a famous ship that was considered unsinkable, and yet the crew crashed the boat into an iceberg, causing it to sink. This kind of tragedy that resulted in the loss of life, product, and hope occurred because of a lack of vision. The crew members neglected their ability to see, and this analogy applies to our real lives now. People don't pay attention to all of the variables that could possibly happen. This is why it is crucial that we have coordinates, and even if they are subject to change, that is okay. There is no value investing in a plan that doesn't exist. Create or sustain a plan, and have tunnel vision that is unbothered. Sometimes the plan is as simple as having an idea and executing one idea over and over until it produces something massive. Focus on your vision; a person who lacks vision will become a follower to another person's vision. That is not good or bad, it just is. Most of us need to step outside of our comfort zone and become the leaders that we need for our own vision; we don't need a hero to guide us.

Broken Home

War in the home, it was you versus me,
She versus you, and us dying every day.

Because we refuse to live,
We refuse to let go of the negativity, so

Another knife gets pulled,
Another child gets abused.

While our addiction to drugs and alcohol
Just push us apart like the tectonic plates

That shifts the state of California
Into the Pacific Ocean.

People on the Outside are Texas.
Meanwhile, we are Los Angeles falling off

Into the fucking abyss of the depth of
This Broken Home, jaded ocean.

—Sylvester McNutt III

Peace after Pain

You start missing a person, and you romanticize about how things could've been. You've been hurt by a relationship falling apart. It could be your friend, your family member, or a distant lover. I suppose the key to all of this is to remember that you'll create a sustainable madness in your head if you continue to fall back into the sadness of the situation. Emotions run wild, tempers may flare as well, but the emotional triggers do not define the situation. Your responses and your actions define the situation. Be very mindful that you do not allow the madness of sadness to ruin progress. It's okay to miss people; it's a normal human process. Just remember that you don't actually miss them, you just miss what they used to represent. Now there is a void, so all I ask you to do for yourself is to fill your time with people you care about, deepen your friendships, and understand that it will be okay. You can obtain peace after pain. In psychology, social coping is the ability to seek support from others. This tactic can be very helpful if the source is trusted friends, roommates or loved ones.

Social Support

Social support can be broken down into four categories:

1. Emotional Support - love, empathy, caring or affection.

2. Tangible Support - emotional support, material goods or financial help.

3. Informational Support - advice or information.

4. Companionship Support – social belonging.

Love is not abuse.

Love is not taking advantage of.

Love is not manipulation

Love is not violence

Love is not war

Love is not walking on eggshells

Love is not feeling alone

Love is not feeling inadequate

Love is not feeling like you're not good enough

None of that is love; do not confuse it.

—Sylvester McNutt III ("Love Hate")

You will overcome everything that is meant to destroy you.

If you keep your heart in the darkness, you will never overcome the things that are meant to destroy you. Your consciousness is always searching for truth, your heart is searching for happiness, and your soul wants to be loved. The only relevant offer for this is to practice self-love, to give your love to others, and to always remain aware of how your actions impact your life.

—Sylvester McNutt III (*Dear Soul*)

Don't get caught up in holding on to negative behaviors that kill and reduce your soul. There's life on the other side of your adversity. Face it, and allow the unknown to become the known. Everything that you know right now was at one point a new experience or new information, so allow the unknown to dominate you.

—Sylvester McNutt III

I Am Not Afraid

We all died from the way life has treated us
They broke us and left us open like the
potholes of an old road in Chicago.
But the twisting motion of those hands that
went around our necks are no longer there.

The stones and brick that were used to bash
our face are no longer there.
The coward who took our sexual benefits
before we even understood our bodies no
longer have power over us.

The person who knocked us unconscious
no longer has the power to hit us.
The person who put us in a coma does not
have the ability to beat us to a pulp.

You're going to be what you set out to be—
fuck everyone who doesn't support the new
you.

You're a winner and a champion, you're
gifted and blessed, and most importantly,
you're not afraid to stand up for yourself.

Dear Soul,

Everyone's life has some type of fall. The fall depicted here through poetry describes different scenes of darkness and abuse that we have all encountered through our different paths.

None of it is fiction, because all of it has been experienced by somebody's soul. It isn't something that we should ignore because our brothers and sisters are walking around carrying this pain. We are carrying this pain, and it is important as a culture that we attack the things that have stressed us out for years.

Fear is natural, and having a confrontation with fear is natural as well. Events from our past will always cause us pain if we do not understand and attempt to face them.

No, we do not have to sit inside of this pain that was caused by these events. So instead of running from the "the falls," or stresses of life, we can enact a conscious effort to overcome or face these things.

If you're a human who currently participates in these behaviors, I urge you to remember the last poem and remember the theme—it says, "I am not afraid."

You do not have to be afraid to walk away from a negative situation. You do not have to be afraid to look yourself deep in the soul, to relive those feelings so you can let them go and return to a healthy state. It is okay to seek professional help, to restart life, and practice new habits that will produce efficient results.

Letting go of all of the things that hurt you is one of the most freeing and enjoyable experiences that we may encounter as a human. It's okay, and you deserve new energy. You do not have to be afraid. You matter, and you're the most important person in this trip called life. Your consciousness lies inside of your cerebral cortex, also known as your advanced brain, and underneath that you'll find the primitive pain that controls our automatic and subconscious actions. Danger signals occur inside of your brain, in the amygdala. The amygdalae trigger physical reactions based on what you see and what you hear. For example, if you're in a movie and you hear a heartbeat, it could trigger a reaction of anxiety because you just know something is going to occur. Our primitive brain cannot tell the difference between fear in a movie and real-life fear.

Your breathing will accelerate, your heart rate will rise, and your pupils will dilate to give you clearer vision. This is what fear does to you from a physical standpoint. Fear like this will make us do one of two things—fight or flight. Fight the stimuli creating the fear, or run from it. The reason we would do either is because of human self-preservation. Self-preservation is the evaluation of a situation and our response to it so we can stay alive and safe. If we want ultimate growth, self-awareness, and self-mastery, then we cannot run from fear. Not the fear of facing the past, not the fear of loving again, or the fear of getting over and letting go of the negative things that slow us down from a progress standpoint. Facing your fear is the most liberating tool you'll ever do. If you were abused as a child, suppressing the thoughts will haunt you. You'll run from talking about it, because fear won't allow you accept it. See, now if you remember everything we've talked about in this chapter, you see that it's starting to come full circle.

The closer, or quicker, that you can get to acceptance, the better. However, the duration that one takes to get to acceptance will vary based on stimuli and processing. Just remember, that is okay.

The fear of the unknown is universal, and it is okay to have fear based on our personal experiences. We learn the fear of heights around six months, and we develop a fear of separation because love and belonging are things we need to be healthy. Outside of those two instances, fear comes from traumatic events. If a dog attacks you when you're a child, you'll fear or dislike dogs forever. I personally do not like dogs, and the reason is because it was enforced to me at a young age that dogs are ruthless animals. See, I have an emotional memory based on dogs, and I'll never get over it until I accept that not all dogs are going to hurt me. This is called *fear conditioning*. This is why we never get over things that hurt us. Fear is normal. Figuring out why and sometimes facing this fear can help us get over it. Acceptance is the key to recovery because it allows us to be free of denial, bargaining, or depression.

I love seeing people

recover from

messed-up situations.

—Sylvester McNutt III

Kids in the Forest and Fear

If two kids got lost in the forest, they wouldn't panic. They would look at each other as each other's savior. They lack the ability to hold fear like adults do, so these kids will take more risks and ask more questions that adults do. Kids have a better chance at escaping the forest than adults. Adults activate fear and distrust, and that's why we stay trapped inside of the tundra. Instead, we need to activate our curiosity and cooperation abilities. We can only reach our purpose and recover from poor situations once we change our feelings about fear.

Fear, is a normal part of life, it is here to protect us from danger. A lot of gurus preach as if fear is not real, and as if it is only an illusion. Unfortunately, that mentality is only a method of propaganda and it is not realistic. Fear can, indeed, disrupt our ability to recover or be successful; fear navigates us away from stimuli that can cause harm.

When you're in the forest of life do not allow fear to keep you from growing; remind yourself, that you need to take more risks. Life is a trip that requires you to get off at destinations when you're not ready; the best moments in life occur after risks and fear have confused you.

Three Steps for the Recovery Trail

Reformation (Step One)

Sometimes the only thing you can do when everything is falling apart around you is to allow it to break. The moment I started to accept things, as they were it allowed me to let go of so much negativity and pressure that wasn't working in favor of my soul. I was seeing a girl who refused to commit to me but she wanted to "chill." At this point in my life, I knew I wanted more, and I needed to be with someone who understood commitment. Her energy was weighing me down and making me feel like I was in the wrong. Once I heard that line, that it was okay to allow things to fall apart, I felt so much lighter. We hold on to so many expectations and fantasies, as I was doing with her, and that was what was killing my happiness. It was the fact that my expectation didn't align with my reality.

All my life I heard quotes about being strong and fighting through whatever process you're dealing with. Especially being a young black man—we get drilled with the idea that you must be strong in order to be valuable.

I grew up confused and never believed that allowing something to die or self-destruct was actually okay. After a while, I started to notice that there was more peace in allowing self-destructive things to implode.

After I heard that quote, I lost my job, my car broke down, and the woman I was talking to said she wanted to leave my life. I'm not going to lie. It was a hard time, but there was growth in that situation for me because I allowed my mind to get closer to acceptance rather than sitting there and keeping my heart stuck in denial or rejection.

One of the most beautiful things you can do is allow damage to be damage. You do not want to mask the pain as love. You have to realistically identify pain as pain so you can treat the stimuli accordingly. The author of *Broken Vision*, Horacio Jones Jr., once stated, "Trust is fragile." I believe that trusting in yourself to recover is more valuable than trusting in the ability of the stimuli to break you. Nothing can break you; you're too bendy for that. Allow things to break so they can reformat your viewpoint. This is your reformation and the path to recovery.

Trusting in yourself to recover

is more valuable than trusting in

the ability of stimuli to break you.

—Sylvester McNutt III ("Trust Thyself")

If a knife fell off the kitchen table,

would you try to grab it?

No, because you don't want to get cut.

Some of the people, jobs,

and situations in your life are knives,

and they keep stabbing you because

you keep reaching.

—Sylvester McNutt III ("No Self-Harm")

Environment (Step Two)

In 2011 I wanted to move away from Chicago because there was a massive amount of growth that I needed as a human, but I never really thought about moving away forever, since I was born and raised in Chicago. My mother and father were both born in Chicago, and my entire family lived there, and of course all of my friends lived there from high school and college, so for me the environment was one that had a lot of expectation and confusion as I tried to grow from what I always knew—but my Chicago associations really wouldn't allow me to grow.

> Sometimes people aren't excited about your
> growth because they only knew you, they don't
> know you now. They just have a slimmer version
> of how you used to be in their head. They don't
> accept you as you are right now. A lot of the times,
> these are the people who are the closet to you.
>
> —Sylvester McNutt III

I had the feeling that most people get when they are complacent and they decide to deal with those emotions—the feeling that something is missing and there needs to be more is an emotion you should always listen to. I dealt with that feeling every single day, and then finally I made a decision. My decision was that I wanted to move out to the West Coast because I felt like my heart belonged in the West. I knew my soul needed new life. In fact, when I was in high school, I wrote my mother a letter telling her that after I finished college, I would relocate to the West Coast and live my life out there.

At the time I was working at Verizon Wireless as a retail sales associate, and I was really good at my job. I was one of the top sales people in my district and area, but it wasn't enough to satisfy my soul cravings. My heart was not settled, and I was often stressed out by the lifestyle I was living. I worked forty to fifty hours per week; I never saw my siblings or friends unless it was a "Sunday Funday" of drinking. Although Sundays with friends can be fun when you feel like you're only living your life for the weekend, the job becomes mundane and almost useless to your happiness.

So I did like most people do who work a lot: I dove deep into my job and got better because, for some reason, when we are not satisfied, we try harder. After two weeks of giving more effort at my job, I figured that if I really applied myself to my craft, I could excel to the next level of management. I applied to California and Arizona every single day. I simply no longer could grow in that environment in Illinois. I applied outside of my company and started taking proactive steps to move my life to Arizona. I started selling and giving away my clothing, furniture, and personal belongings.

Honestly, I never visited Arizona or California, but I knew I needed a change, so I meditated on it and willed it to happen with my consistent action. After months of interviews and patience I landed a promotion with my company in Phoenix, Arizona. Even though I had a girlfriend, family, and a good job in Chicago, it wasn't enough to satisfy my soul at that point because none of it felt right. I knew my life needed change, because I wasn't growing anymore. I am a creative person, and at the time I didn't have any opportunity to create anything.

I was just a clone, and I wanted more freedom to explore my dear soul. Through my hard work, I was extended an offer to join the management team at one of the Arizona retail locations. So I subleased my apartment and sold all of my furniture. I had saved up $6,000 and left with whatever would fit in my car. I was twenty-five, and I was largely unaware of what my life was going to be like once I arrived in Arizona.

My friend said he wanted to drive across the country with me, so once I finished my last shift in Illinois, we hit the road. Brandon slept when I drove and vice versa. The drive across the country was the most relaxing and enlightening experience because I was alone with the stars for most of the night driving.

A lot of people are terrified to make that risk, or feel like because of their great job or kids they are rooted. People are spirits; we can be wherever we want. One of the things that helped fuel me was the passing of my grandmother in March that year. There's no way that she would've wanted me to stay in an environment that I was not happy with. So in turn, death became life for me. She passed in March, and I left in September for Arizona and never looked back.

Mind-set (Step Three)

These steps do not have to occur in order. They are just things that I've noticed that help. Some people will suggest that you simply change your mind, which for me was impossible when in Chicago. I had to leave my environment before I could really shift my mind. I feel like the influential forces of people you've known or have been around are too great to really make the change you want by saying, "I'm just going to focus on xyz." For example, I notice that people never keep their New Year's resolutions, and I feel like it's because you're around the same people, so the behavior will remain the same because the support is the same. However, when you take a vacation and have an experience that changes your behavior when you return, the absence of self shows people that you've grown. I'll give you a real-world example that I experienced.

When I moved to Arizona from Chicago, I took all the same behaviors and mindsets. I was a massive meat eater. In Chicago all we do is eat meat-lovers' pizza, hot dogs, and burgers. The best thing to eat in Chicago is fried chicken—we do that well there. However, I became a vegetarian and adopted a plant-based diet that I believe will never leave my side. I couldn't become that until I changed my environment. It was really easy to become successful in that department when I didn't have people around me who had meat-eating expectations. I was able to navigate my choices freely without conflict from criticism for making different choices than the crowd. So as you grow, I want you to pay attention to the environment and mind-sets—they have a working relationship with each other.

Your mind-set and your environment always have a direct correlation with your outcome. Here's a practical example. One of my best friends is a man who objectifies women without any awareness of what he is doing. Now, I am not saying that something is wrong with this behavior. I'm not judging the behavior. I'm simply observing the outcome, and the following observation creates conflict. He claims that he wants to get a wife and have a family. In psychology there's a term called *cognitive dissonance*, which refers to a person who has conflict in a scenario because this individual's action does not align with his or her mind-set. This situation is strictly about conflicting attitudes inside of a person. The actual state of cognitive dissonance is the inconsistency between thoughts or believes that a person currently holds.

If you ever go on the Internet, you'll see quotes that say, "Just give me consistency." In psychology, consistency is called a "consonance." We naturally search for the consonance because it gives us peace within our thought processes. My friend believes that he can continue to completely objectify women, and somehow he thinks this will lead him to actually find a wife. Granted, in relationship situations, people change their mind-sets as the situations and environments change, but I do not see how a man in this generation could actually commit intimately, emotionally, and sexually to a woman if he completely objectifies her.

For the sake of establishing a baseline, to me, the objectification of a woman means to see her as a sexual object whose purpose is to be used as a sexual retreat or as a participant in a sexual fantasy. I've had this male brain for a long time—some people do not have the awareness to really understand what their brain and/or self really does.

We are taught to grade ourselves, and everything is about comparison. *Dear Soul* is about intrinsic observations and really understanding self. If I see my "type" of woman, then I instantly fantasize about her subconsciously. Even if it's just for a second, the fantasy occurs, and for the sake of a baseline, I believe that even looking at and observing her beauty is a fantasy behavior. With my friend, he takes the art of objectification to the next level. First, he doesn't just notice women. He gawks at them and looks at them like they're objects. He does it in a way that is so low and disguising that the entire concept of "a woman loving him" seems completely egregious because his actions and his cognition do not align with the his thoughts and perceptions at all. Now, I want you to be very careful when making your observations, because you need to be mindful of the subjective information that you add to your observations. With my experience and education and observations of others, I literally believe it is impossible for a man to love a woman with a mind-set that objectifies her into his sexual fantasy alone. I'm not making the claim that a man cannot love a woman if he objectifies her. I am saying that if he only objectifies her, then he cannot truly love her. Love is not something that lives inside of the objectification or perception of ownership.

Yes, couples do sexual role-plays and fantasies, but those are successful after a baseline of respect has been established and understood by both parties. Always remember that from a scientific point of view, we really can't observe cognitive dissonance—it's something that exists, but you can only become aware of it. You can measure and observe a substance like water or iron, but cognitive dissonance is a purely internal phenomenon, so it's immeasurable, but that doesn't mean it's not occurring.

In the instance of my friend, he doesn't have a consonance because his desire of finding a wife (cognition) and his behavior of internally and externally objectifying women (dissonance) do not align. So now we find ourselves in a situation that *all* people come across. This is the moment where you have to deal with the cognitive dissonance, but we typically don't know how.

First, you must acknowledge what you can and cannot control in every environment. On a deep psychological level, you can influence and manipulate other people, but ultimately you can only control your perception and expression of your feelings.

Changing Attitude or Behavior (Cognitive Dissonance Solutions)

In the situation I named above with my friend who claims he wants a wife, but only objectifies women, there are actually two people having dissonance in that situation. I am one of them, and he is the other. I explained his dissonance to him. However, he is unaware of it, so he will continue his ways until an external force pushes him to change, because he is unaware of it. And the change cannot come internally if you're not aware of the problem.

I also have cognitive dissonance because I feel like I have the answer, and I keep trying to give a solution to a person who does not even want the answer to the question. Previously, I wasn't aware of my own participation in the cognitive dissonance, until I decided to step back and perceive the situation with an objective viewpoint versus the subjective one I had previously.

After I removed myself from the situation, I saw that there were only two outcomes:

1. My friend will continue to use and objectify women, and he won't find his wife.

2. My friend will continue to use and objectify women, and he will find his wife.

See, it's not my business to switch the behavior expectation, because that's not reality. As of today, he only objectifies women, so why should I give him the benefit of the doubt that it would change? That doesn't make any sense to me at all. There are also two outcomes for the other subject in the cognitive dissonance, which is me, and here are my options:

1. I can keep observing my friend and continue to get upset and relay information that he is not ready for, causing me more conflict because I do not understand why he is saying one thing and doing another.

2. I can remove my perception and subjective viewing of his actions and accept him as he is, and in turn remove my emotional attachment to his outcomes.

In conclusion, this chapter is the most relevant because it sets the building blocks for all of the topics that I cover in the book. This chapter is so deep, however, it covers all the tools we need to be successful, to let go, and to grow as an individual. I'm sitting among the conflict and cognitive dissonance every day because I cannot understand my friend and his cognitive dissonance. However, what solution did I offer? What steps did I offer in the beginning of this chapter around grieving and moving forward?

Switching your mind-set may change your life.

Keeping the same environment while

attempting

to switch your mind is growth paralysis.

Your growth may be an illusion.

—Sylvester McNutt III ("Illusion")

You must enjoy murder, since you willingly go back into situations that kill your soul daily—that's called soul suicide.

Instead of forcing your input and ideas upon others, just sit back and observe. Your soul can live better inside of observation versus jumping in and out of these situations.

—Sylvester McNutt III ("Soul Suicide")

Environment Switch

It does not make you weak if you leave a situation that you've tried your best in and it still is not producing blissful results. Life is short. I don't believe in beating a dead horse. The hard part of life is accepting that sometimes you have to let go of people, titles, and some of the mind-sets you currently have in order to be happy.

Stimuli that breaks your spirit is often just an illusion. The real power is in knowing that the stimulus is not breaking us; the power lies within.

True power will always reside in knowing that the recovery to every situation will always occur from within. Healing, moving on, and letting go are all internal processes.

My soul acquired more peace once I stopped reacting to everything that occurred in my life.

—Sylvester McNutt III

Dear Soul,

If you know that you have anger or resentment building up, I challenge you to make a difference and to make a change with the stimuli that is causing the anger. I would like you to accept that you are the source, because you are allowing something external to impact you.

Depending on where you are within your path consciousness will determine how your perception of anger or stress will impact your current mood. If there is something pushing against you, causing you stress and pain, then the challenge is to figure out something about yourself.

Are you able to remove your emotional attachment to this situation or person causing you the problem?

If you are able to remove yourself, then it's much easier to get away from, but if it's a situation where you cannot get away from the pain, then you have to look at your perception of it.

Eight Daily Tips to Recover from Negativity

1. Delete all the songs, movies, and media that could remind you of the stimuli.

2. Listen to or watch media that provides you positive energy.

3. Don't blame anyone for what they do, especially yourself.

4. Find forgiveness for the people who have harmed you.

5. Create new environments, with new energy that does not remind you of the past.

6. Watch or attend a live comedy show. The laughter will help you lean toward happiness.

7. Unfollow, delete, and block each person working against your recovery.

8. Never lose hope that you deserve different.

We miss the best moments

because we pull out our phone

and try to take a picture of it.

Nothing compares to the present

moment. Sit back and observe

life. It's a wonderful dream.

—Sylvester McNutt III

SHE IS THAT READY

The women in this generation need a voice and a representation outside of their own selves because they are often not heard. *Dear Soul* and Sylvester McNutt III will attempt to be their voice.

I hate the way society is set up right now, because our women are violated, used, and abused. Not just by men, but also by each other, by corporations and standards of beauty, which are unrealistic and ridiculous.

Women compete with women and destroy each other in the gym, at jobs, and across social media. It's so ugly to me that in my last book, *The Dear Queen Journey*, I talked about how women calling each other *bitch* was so ugly to me and how they should stop doing it. It's a very disgusting world to raise a daughter in right now. We are teaching our daughters to fear men, hate women, and to hate their own selves.

I want you to always treat me like I'm your big brother. I'm not going to lie in my art, and my only purpose is to create thought and spark awareness. You may not agree with what I say, but my words are not here for agreement. They exist to ignite a fire in people. I'm here to say the things we talk about in our living rooms and with our friends, and to give voice to those feelings we have but cannot put into words.

Men do what women allow us to do. If you make fun of other women or put them down, then that same treatment will come from a man or, even worse, other women. I remember when I was a kid and all the girls I hung out with told me, "I can't stand hanging out with girls. I like boys so much better because it's just less drama."

As a young boy I never understood this, but as I'm now aware of this as an adult, I am able to really see that our women have a deep-rooted psychological problem that pushes them to feel like everything is a competition among them.

If you're reading this book from the female perspective, I challenge you to start a woman's empowerment group, a female book club, or some kind of women's organization in your neighborhood.

I challenge you to take real world steps to lift each other up, and I will support the movement. I have a huge network on social media, and I will support any of you who do this, if it's genuine. My purpose is to spark the brain of the people who are going to change the world, and that is *you*!

Fellas, we have to stop marginalizing the true power of our women. We must start glorifying our male role models and allow the negative ones to stop getting famous. I want the little girls of this culture to have a fighting chance to grow into healthy, happy women. This chapter is dedicated to understanding our women and lifting them up. Our women are "that ready."

WE

MUST

HEAL

OUR

WOMEN

The only question I have for her is, why does she sit up at night scrolling her text messages threads, looking at social media and comparing her life to others?

She just wants to level up her spirituality, her health, and her love life.

So why does she keep scrolling? None of that stuff will happen inside of that cell phone.

That cell phone is a toxic tool if you're looking to find anything of substance.

Let it go. Don't be like the rest of this generation.

—Sylvester McNutt III

She gave her love away

To people who didn't

care to understand romance.

Now she understands

That she doesn't have

An ordinary love.

—Sylvester McNutt III ("Ordinary")

Nine Steps to Love Your Woman Deeper

1. Write her a poem. She will appreciate knowing that you took the time to sit down and craft something creative for her.

2. Look her directly in the eye when she speaks so she knows that you are taking in what she is saying.

3. Send her a long e-mail or text message while she is asleep so when she wakes up she knows that you were thinking of her.

4. Find out how she likes to be touched and do that, and then innovate it as she grows.

5. Don't make her look stupid for choosing you. Women put a lot of their emotions into picking the "right" guy, so it can be very draining to her if she feels like she made an error.

6. One of the most important things you can do is take the time to care about what she is saying. She will feel so much better once she knows you're trying to get her.

7. Have a plan. Do not just go with the flow of everything. You need to have a plan for her heart. She'll love knowing that there is direction in the relationship.

8. Feed her as often as possible. Put her around food, or talk about food with her. Women love food.

9. Find ways to compliment her on the way she makes you feel. She will want to do it more and feel more valued.

She overcame

Everything

That was meant

To destroy her.

—Sylvester McNutt III ("She's That Ready")

Honestly, her body is tired and her soul is even more tired. She is ready to build a future, to build herself, and to build you up. She is tired of the games, the issues, and the conflict. She wants to get to know someone, the real person, without the truth being withheld. She's that ready.

—Sylvester McNutt III ("She's That Ready")

She wants the next one she gets to

know to be the last one she gets to know.

She is that ready.

—Sylvester McNutt III ("She's That Ready")

Woman of Passion

As a man, you cannot be afraid of a woman of passion. If you're calling her crazy, it means that you don't understand her. Yes, she will hold you accountable. No, it won't be easy to get her attention. She is a woman who will love you deeper than any ocean. She will uplift her man, but she will do everything from her core. Her heart defines her. She is a woman of passion, and there is nobody like her. She is the type to give everything that she has; a woman of passion will multiply every environment she enters. Her purpose is love; she gives it with no equivocations. This is the type of woman that wars are fought over, she will kill any doubt you've ever had about real love. A woman of passion only knows how to love with all of her soul. Her love is intense, it like pushing the moon closer to the earth. Her love is like the sun, as it reaches through the entire universe giving life to all of the organisms that it touches. A woman of passion will not settle for love that is hidden or uncommitted. She has seen the depths of displacement and now her purpose is love; she is the most valuable player for your team. If you want to put together a championship string, you'll need to figure out how to love a woman of passion correctly. Learn how to hold her to alleviate her stress, and learn how to make her feel like she is the most important person to you. Her love is multiplied when she knows your focus is dialed in on her.

—Sylvester McNutt III

I love a woman

Of passion; she puts

Her heart into

Everything.

—Sylvester McNutt III

She may not have all of the answers, but she is asking the

questions. She may not be perfect based on this society's perspective of what perfect is, but I reassure you that there are no such thing as flaws.

Her power is more than anything. She will not settle for

something that is not everything. She is everything, so she needs her life to be equal to, or greater than, that, and she doesn't expect everyone to understand this path, but she does expect them to understand that she is That Ready.

Every opportunity she has to give love, she will. She is like the

sun that sits in the middle of our universe, exerting her power, hoping that the universe grows from her energy. As the sun gives nutrition and light to the solar system, so does she. Her light is the light that turns cold nights into warm days and terrible moods into modules of love. If you find a queen like her, grow with her and cherish her, because there aren't many like her.

—Sylvester McNutt III

Workplace

She is frustrated with the fact that the way society is set up, she has to make less money than a man. It's irrational and disrespectful to marginalize her capabilities simply because of her gender. That doesn't make any sense or cents to her. She went to college too, she has business savvy too, and she is powerful too. So it needs to be fair. Women are exhausted from feeling like they have to flirt or allow sexual harassment in the workplace just to advance. Men can be assholes and have no problems getting promoted, but she has to fit the standard and play games. She is tired of that, and she is that ready for a change. No, she doesn't want to teach her daughter this psychological nonsense to advance in the workplace. Women are CEOs too, women are managers, and they are hard workers. Women shouldn't have to lose their jobs or paychecks because they have children. Motherhood is a very important feature of life, and she should have job protection once it occurs. She shouldn't have to come back six weeks later. As a culture, we need to demand these corporations and the government enact laws that protect our women for at least the first year of motherhood. We need to give women the "right" and "chance" to raise a child without the stress of going back to work early.

Dear Single Mother Soul,

Don't cry yourself to sleep anymore. There is nothing wrong with you, and no man can negate your worth as a woman.

You were lucky enough to have the honor of motherhood, and that is worthy of a trophy. You carried a child. You're raising that child and wearing multiple hats right now to support and care for that child. Dating may seem a little bit harder in your position because you can't just bring anyone around your kids. I agree, but don't you for one second think that having kids negates the possibilities of love that can meander through your soul.

Make sure you tie up the loose ends and try to create a situation with the father in which communication is respectful and cordial. Once that is accomplished, go through your grieving and healing process as needed. Remember, the number one thing you need to be healthy is acceptance. Accept that you and your child's father will not be together anymore, and most importantly let go of any expectation of him. The expectations will stress you out and kill your view of reality. Yes, of course we should expect him to be a father to his kids, but we also expected him to stay around and be committed to you, right? Regardless, what happened did, so instead of focusing on the negativity, I am urging you to let it go. Let's save your soul the stress, and let's remove any expectation, and let's live in acceptance.

You're going to think about him, and that is normal and okay. All you have to do is realize that the main reason you think about an ex is because he represents love to you. Since you're currently craving love, it makes sense that you would think of the last person who represented it. Let go, move on, and develop a stream of communication and respect. Do not argue with him; do not try to make him look like an idiot; just take the high road. Understand that his only role is to father his kids now, so if he's accepted that, work with him.

Your kids are sponges and will repeat what they see, so be very careful of your messages and how you communicate around them. If you're bitter, hostile, and upset, your sons and daughters will become what they see. You're an adult; always take accountability and the high road.

The most important thing you can do is let go of things you cannot control and allow new energy to come into your life. Don't worry about all the negative toxic energy from the past. Let it go.

Stop leaving our women out here to raise children alone; it takes two to create a child. If you do not want to develop a relationship with her, that's fine, but she wants to raise a healthy child, and *she is that ready*. Put the pettiness aside, and let's raise our children.

Understand that nobody can replace the father. Part of being a man is taking care of your responsibility as a man. Remember, sons will typically model their father's behavior, and daughters will seek men similar to their father. With that being said, never give up on your children. That is too much of a risk to take; it's your responsibility to raise your children and your vibration.

Being a mom is a blessing; she is not upset with that at all. She doesn't understand how a man can participate in the creation of a child and then be absent in the existence of the child.

Single Mom

There's nothing wrong with you.
You are not any less valuable because
You have a child; do not ever think
Or say those words aloud.
Do not give up hope that you
Will one day find a king who will
Appreciate you and your child.

You're raising a child; you're growing yourself. Your job is not easy, because you wear more than one hat. There are things you don't understand, but you keep on ticking. Your passion levels are at an all-time high, but your patience is low. You don't have patience for negativity or conflict from others. You have a lot of questions, and not all the answers. Some days are harder than others, I know, but just remember those days when you look over and see your child. That joy you get when you see your kid is reason enough to keep going. Children are a blessing; they need you to constantly evolve and grow as a person too. It's okay not to have the right answer; it's okay to make mistakes. Do not eat yourself up because you feel like you made poor decisions; let yourself breathe and escape any type of negative self-talk. You're not just a mother; you're a spiritual leader, a role model, and the most important person in someone's life. Do not forget this.

Axiom

She is the sun that always shines

The taxes that are always collected.

Gravity pulls people down but her love

is the most uplifting force to others.

Like an escalator, she is the reason,

The moment, and the truth.

She is an Axiom.

—Sylvester McNutt III

She wanted to speak about the universe,

the moon, and equality. I just sat there,

proud, and listened as she spewed her

soul to me. Little does she know that a

woman of passion is my weakness.

—Sylvester McNutt III

Not a Joke

She shouldn't have to conceal her sexuality simply because people do not have self-control. She's frustrated with the constant objectification of her body. It feels like people think she is a piece of meat that can just be ordered off a menu. The harassment that goes on in the work place, on social media, and in this culture is a disservice to her self-awareness. Our women are growing up with an overdeveloped understanding of their insecurities, but there is not a single outlet addressing *why* and *where* these insecurities are coming from. I will not raise my daughter to think that it is "okay" to have her entire being reduced to someone's sexual desire. My daughter will know that she can do anything; her hip-to-waist ratio will not define her. As a culture, we need to sit down and have realistic conversations with our daughters about this unrealistic culture. As men, we have to talk to our boys about what sexual harassment is and appropriate ways to make sexual passes at women. We are all human. Sexual thoughts and advances are indeed normal, but if it's done to the extent of being rude or has an underlying message of fear, then it needs to be corrected. We have to teach our young boys how to read and understand if a woman is not interested in our sexual passes. We have to teach our little girls how to stand up for how they feel, because sexual harassment is not a joke. With more empathy and understanding we can raise awareness and change this behavior. Let's all have these conversations at out coffee tables.

Dear Soul,

There is a valuable lesson to be learned inside the struggle of another person. My perspective of life is through the eyes of a man, through the eyes of a black person, and through the eyes of a person who has seen the depths of hell and the heights of heaven. I was born in Chicago, Illinois, and I am a person who is well traveled. This is solely a self-reflection of my perspective and awareness of self. There are things that I am largely unaware of. Let's be honest—I've never been a woman, I've never been rich, and I've never lived outside of the country, so my perspective is limited to that experience.

While I was writing this book, my friend asked, "What makes you an authority to speak for women?" My answer: empathy.

I am not a woman; I am a man. I have the ability to align with and understand other people's pain. I understand struggle because I come from struggle. If a woman speaks up for feminism, which is the movement to support equality among genders, she will be told to sit down. We men can speak up for them, this is called "shared equality." I live in male privilege but have the ability to speak up for what my female counterparts go through. The same thing applies for race. If I make this entire book about uplifting black people, it won't have the impact I want. I am looking to shift the culture. I need all men to speak up for women. More importantly, I need my male readers to align with our female counterparts. The same applies to all races. We need to understand each other and align. The sexism, racism, and separation that goes on in this generation is exactly why we have problems.

Remember that separation causes all conflict; our souls and energies are always connected. Do not feel like our skin color separates us from feeling pain or joy; we are the same beings. Later on in this book I am going to address the Black Lives Matter movement. I am a black person, and the actions that prompted this movement really upset me. I am allowed to empathize and align with other humans' pain. Empathy is the number one trait needed to turn us into beings who can efficiently participate in a community. Community awareness and participation is the key to success; we all need to feel connected to loving people. The most important things I want you to take away from this letter is that empathy is gold, aligning is silver, and understanding another person's point of view is bronze. All of those traits are necessary to have a championship mind-set. Which medal, or medals, do you own?

Shared Equality

We are all human; we have one race.

We need more empathy for our journeys.

Less judgment of each other and

More acceptance is the only way to heal

This culture. Let's commit to speaking up

For the equality of our fellow human being.

It will require a little more selfishness; it will

Require that we let go of our prejudices as often as

Possible and just accept people as they are.

THOUGHTS OF AN ADDICT

Becoming Aware of Addictions

Hair feeling real heavy, she stood still as the ocean pushes out wind that goes up and down her spine like the vertebrae that holds her upright. She's trapped in the killing field of feeling real. Damn, she doesn't know how deep this rabbit hole goes, so she pops another pill and has sex with another guy whose name she cannot recall. She is ready for the fall, but her bloodstream stays so lit that she can't even process the idea of something else.

He resorts to violence because he was beat as a child. His environment was nothing but vixens and bruisers, so acting "hard" and slaying women is not a big deal to him. It is culture. He lies to women for sex because the game of attracting them runs his anxiety away just like the bottles that he always finishes. He grabs a bottle every day because he just needs to escape the stress of his job and life. He is ready for a fall but isn't even aware of it.

They keep putting up more money for the cause because the people keep beating against them. They love the feeling that goes off in their brain when they secure another victory. These people are addicted to the dopamine that goes off every time they make a bet and win.

These addictions are killing us every single day because most of the time we are not even aware of them. We do not become aware of our addiction to watching six hours of television a night. We are not aware of the alcohol bottles that we consume every night until we lose or regular consciousness.

People who are addicts often times appear as high-functioning citizens of the culture. They have jobs and are oftentimes in positions of leadership. Leadership makes you go crazy. It makes you responsible for things that you cannot control. This is why parents go mad once they realize their kids have minds of their own and they cannot control the children.

A lot of parents aren't ready for that pressure. People popping these Adderall pills aren't ready for the static of life. Alcoholics run to the bottom of bottles because those moments of dehydration, slurred words, and dysfunction make them feel alive.

You're not ready for a fall—you're on the fucking fall, and you're losing control of your life every single day that you do not focus on yourself. If you're addicted, you know that you have an addiction deep inside, but the majority of the time your addictions are attached to a chemical reaction in your brain that forces you to become a slave to the stimulus.

Cell phone, social media, and feedback addicts need the dopamine that gets triggered from notifications, because it makes them feel alive and loved. They love dopamine because dopamine makes them feel like they belong and that they are accepted. Typically, addictions are not sacrificed cold turkey. In my honest opinion, I believe that a healthy person who can acknowledge and become self-aware of an addiction can correct the behaviors around it. I also do not believe having an addiction makes you an unhealthy person. Healthy is relative to the persons and the impact they have on the lives around them, including their own, obviously.

The addiction that I have a direct relationship with is alcoholism, because both of my parents were alcoholics. I am not, nor have I been, an alcoholic. However, alcoholism ruined my life from an early child-development perspective. My father eventually stopped drinking after he became disabled and after his health took a turn for the worse. Then he eventually died once a pneumonia attack dominated his lungs. My mother still drinks every day and doesn't realize how damaging the alcohol is to not only her but to those around her—her children and family members.

I don't hold back anymore in my writing. This might be too deep and too hard for some people to read, but again, my only purpose for what I do is to help people. I want us all to be able to grow and learn from these situations. If this subject hits close to home, swallow it some more because we have to suffocate and choke on these thoughts. The only way to increase and deepen our awareness of self and others around us is to have tough conversations with our inner core and the people we interact with. Without awareness and acknowledgment, we will always perish as a culture from a lack of understanding self.

Both of my parents were alcoholics. My father died at the age of fifty, and my mother's soul died many years ago. I haven't known my mother in years and I have no relationship with her today. I haven't had parents since I was a child. By the time I turned thirteen, my parents were gone, and they were just victims of their choices. Two souls who once had a lot of love for each other but allowed their petty ways to cause a chasm between them and their kids.

I am not writing to obtain pity; I have healed and understand the situation. I am sharing this part of my life because I know *Dear Soul* can be used as a preventative tool, as a resource to heal and to help understand. I'm sharing these intimate stories to better the culture for hundreds of years to come. I write these words because there are people who will buy this book, and this is me kicking them right in the chest to tell them to put the alcohol down, to put the petty mind-sets down, and to love these children that you've created.

This is the moment you run out of gas, and the person who picks you up to take you twenty miles to the nearest gas station is a racist, a person who reeks of body odor. Yes, *Dear Soul* wants you to get very uncomfortable. The unknown and the uncomfortable are the main phases we need for personal growth. If this topic makes you that uncomfortable, like it would sitting next to that person I described, then I challenge you to sit inside of the adversity of that uncomfortable feeling.

If any of my family reads this, I hope you understand that my words are not here to appease you or save face to their legacy. At the end of the day, I do have love for my parents, and I will never try to paint a picture of them as if they were wrong or evil. They were and are not that. However, their actions have impacted me and my brothers and sisters. I do not intend to offend. I am only here for the truth, and if you knew my father, he didn't raise me to have a lack of integrity, so I just have to be honest and transparent. Remember that when you read this journey journal called *Dear Soul*, you should look at it as a journal I'm writing to myself for myself.

The unknown and the uncomfortable are the

only mountains that will lead us to

sustainable personal growth. Once we attempt

to climb these rigorous journeys, then and

only then will we gain our new lives.

—Sylvester McNutt III

Five Questions about Hitting Children

1. How do you feel when your boss at work forces you to do something and you cannot do anything about it?

2. If the mind-set is that we must hit our kids when they mess up in order for them to learn, what if that principle was applied to you? For example, if you were late to work instead of calling in, and lying about your lack of planning, what if you had a professional boxer there to hit you in the chest every time you were late? How would that make you feel?

3. Is it possible to teach people by helping them learn from their observations, or is the only solution physical force?

4. What if our role as parents is not to instill discipline via force but to instill deep thought, self-reflection, and self-awareness within our children?

5. Most importantly, what if we are wrong? What if we are making a mistake? What if we stopped looking at disciplining our kids based on a scale that weighs between right and wrong? What if we just needed to observe and reflect versus acting and responding?

In conclusion, I do not believe in objectifying and pushing violence toward people we claim we love. Love does not live inside of violence. Plants can feel our emotions as soon as we come near them, so what about our children who come from us? Imagine what they can feel. I believe that once you demand more self-love from yourself and sit down with your logic on the topic, I believe it will change. I think it is impossible to read these words here and be ignorant and hardheaded to think violence is still an option.

Empathy is the ability to feel another person's pain, and I want you to truly feel the pain you're displacing on your children once you strike them. If you were beat as a child and you continued this behavior as an adult, it is because you were conditioned to this behavior and you believe it is acceptable based upon your past experiences.

I'm not sure of your age, race, or sex, but when I think about hitting my children, I think about what the slaves in America experienced when their slave owners sat on horses and whipped them with leather ropes. I think about what a rape victim feels like when he or she is laying there, hopeless and empty. The last thing I think about is how every single time I was beaten by my father, my mother would stand by without a reaction or intervention.

I remember how I wanted them to die every waking second of every day. This is why I do not believe in child abuse. This is why there is no reasonable justification for hitting a child and why my children will live in a violence-free environment. If you keep hitting your children, they will grow up with unresolved grief and traumatic experiences, so deciding to stop the violence is up to you.

How does this section make you feel? I urge you to sit and write your own personal notes on the subject matter. The next four poems were written throughout my life on this subject, as it is something that I dealt with through my entire life. These entries are titled based on the age I was when I wrote them. Please take time to sit with each one of them and reflect. I wrote them from a child's perspective. You'll see the growth and depth of each poem as I aged. I found a lot of value in retaining all of my notebooks, as they helped me physically see growth and maturation, which we often do not receive tangible references to observe.

92

10

I do not like violence.

Why do the people

who love me,

show me hate?

I don't understand.

Maybe one day I'll

wake up from the madness

and this dirty dream will be

replaced with hugs and kisses.

16

Every single day I would come

home from practice.

Like a boxer, I would get

my ass whooped.

I didn't understand why it was

war in our zone.

I wanted my family to lose me

like *Home Alone*.

Why was it us versus us?

It should've been us versus them.

19

No desire to speak to my parents.

No desire to be in a relationship.

What is the point if it's all just pain?

They never apologized for the

hurricane.

The displacement has me feeling like,

"What's the point of living when your

life has no love?"

This is where I am. I'm not sure if I will

make it to twenty-five, because every

time I look in their eyes, I just see my

suicide. I see it happening...these

visions come to me at night, and that is

why I don't like to sleep anymore.

27

Dear Soul,

I love myself.

I love my kids.

I do not want to be

A source of pain for them.

I will continue to learn and develop

So that they never have to see me as an oppressor.

I want my kids to see me as a source of leadership, a

person that they can always talk to, and most

importantly I want to have their back.

They need to know that they can

Achieve anything they work at.

I will not box them in.

I will not hit my kids.

No violence.

I promise.

—Sylvester McNutt III

WE

MUST

HEAL

OUR

CHILDREN

How to Get Out of a Toxic Situation

I sat at this job, and I wanted to leave so bad, I didn't know how I was going to quit my job, but I knew I needed to go.

I was going to a job that wasn't giving me time to work on my health, because I was clocking over sixty hours per week. My romantic relationship was terrible because I never invested time, and even worse my number one passion, which is writing, was being neglected.

I was making $75,000 per year, but every cent earned pushed me closer to death.

Damn, I knew at this pace I wouldn't survive long, because I used to deal with depression. I knew that this was going to push me into depression if I didn't take action immediately.

So first I bought a new notebook because I wanted to restart my writing career, and next I signed up for a gym membership.

I started going to the gym, but it wasn't enough, because I wasn't eating right, so I started taking my lunch to work and stopped eating out. I started watching documentaries on Netflix about nutrition, and this spurred a desire to really seek knowledge that would help me create and sustain a healthy lifestyle. The next thing I did was epic. I had a realistic conversation with myself about if I could grow and achieve what I wanted while staying in that relationship that wasn't good for her or me anymore.

I knew I had to leave, but I was so weak at that point that I felt like I couldn't let her leave because she was all I had, and that was based on what she was telling me. She

99

wanted to be out of it too, but she literally told me, "I would rather struggle with you and be like this versus going back out into the dating world." When you first hear that line, it sounds poetic, but it's actually very weak minded and represents a person who is okay with codependency.

Codependency is nothing but destruction when it comes to relationships. Codependency is when one person becomes dependent upon the other person for their emotional happiness and identity as a human being. It's a situation where one person supports or enables an addiction, dysfunction, or irresponsibility. She exhibited an excessive need for me to approve of her and had a massive need for me to give her a sense of identity. She was trying to be defined by our relationship, and to me our relationship wasn't even present because the arguing, the accusations, and the pressure did not feel like love at all. It felt like lust and attachment.

This is a descriptive summary of what happened when I needed to escape a toxic situation. If you look closely, you'll see that I actually described three toxic situations:

1. The relationship
2. The job
3. The ailing health

In my observations, when humans suffer, they suffer holistically. This is why we don't recover; this is why we stay trapped in these environments. On the next page I am going to offer you some realistic steps and solutions to get out of toxic situations.

Getting out of toxic situations is about being honest with yourself first. The next step is about taking action over and over and over again until you find yourself out of it.

To get out of a toxic situation you have to accept that you may end up walking a path alone. If you're down and out, being alone doesn't sound that bad versus staying around things that are hurting you. It's going to be okay; never give up the quest to recover.

Twelve Realistic Steps to Get Out of a Toxic Situation

1. Don't ever talk like a victim; be real with yourself about what is happening.

2. Don't make excuses for your job, your environment, or other people's behaviors that impact you. You have to see clearly, and the only way you can do that is by accepting their behaviors.

3. Have realistic expectations of your escape route once you decide it's time to go. In some cases you'll need to create a plan and start executing it before you can actually leave it.

4. Do not talk negatively about yourself; do not feel like you cannot do it. Doubt and negative self-talk will kill all methods of progress and may lead you to start hating yourself.

5. Have a deep understanding of the fears that you're going to have to face in order to take these steps, because fear will stop all progress.

6. Create a realistic plan that will help you leave the situation.

7. Execute the plan, but adjust as you go, because nothing will go as smoothly as you thought.

8. Write down some new healthy barriers that you'd like to set in place. The majority of the time we find ourselves in toxic situations it's because we allow them and we do not set standards for how we are going to be treated.

9. Join a support group or enlist resources from people who have done what you're

attempting to do. Now, be very mindful of the source because the source could be out just for profit or to stir shit up. Either way, do your homework, and make sure this source is actually going to benefit your specific goal.

10. Be mindful of what you post on social media or put out into the public forum. You could create a blog or social media site just to document your journey, but when you do this, be very mindful of your identity and audience. If you're trying to leave an ex and your common friends are on there, it won't work out. If you're trying to lose weight and you create a blog to post your meals, that may help you immensely.

11. Don't hang on to things that have proven to you that they are trying to let go of you. The hardest part of letting go is the fact that we think about all this time and we feel as if we've wasted it. I urge you not to think that way, because every second of that time was valuable information, but with life there is death, and with a rise there must be a fall. Those are axioms for life, and the quicker we accept it, the quicker we grow.

12. Never give up your goal, but be smart enough to reinvent the behaviors around recovering. You may need professional help and guidance. Do not be afraid to ask for help. Pushing your pride aside and asking for help will save you time and emotional stability.

Hanging ON

Why hold on to something that is trying to release its grip? You sit here and squeeze with both hands using all of your muscles, but what you're holding on to is hope. Meanwhile, they're hoping that both hands become sweaty so the grip can slip and result in both of you falling to your emotional death. You can't save a person or anything that is not reaching with all its energy—fuck that. Learn when to let go of negative behaviors, viewpoints, and people; this thought will save your life. Never forget it.

How to Move On after a Breakup

The first step to moving on from bad relationships, negative behavior, or a toxic relationship is to **make a decision**. Without making a firm decision, you'll just waste years and years of your life living a counterfeit fantasy. Wake up, take control of your life, and make a decision.

—Sylvester McNutt III

In order to move on, after you've made a decision to move on, you must define what it means to move on. Until then you will be lost every single second of this process.

The very first step in getting over a situation is to define what it means to move to the next level. In the realm of dating, you'll never be able to get over your ex if you do not clearly define what it means to get over your ex.

In matters of success, if you do not cut ties with negative interactions and determine the parameters of productivity for your interactions, you'll continue to attract the results that you do not want.

When I was playing football, one of my main goals was to become the best at my position on my team. I had a clearly defined goal, which was "be the best at my position on my team."

I wasn't just aimlessly walking around without a purpose. A lot of people want to move on from something, but they've never even addressed the answer to the question of, "What am I moving on to?"

Friends and people who have not read *Dear Soul* will give you advice, such as, "Go have sex with another person" or "Just get a better job," and that is ridiculous. Do not take that advice, because it is terrible and it will continue the void that you already have. It will make it deeper and deeper.

Getting over your ex does not

mean removing him or her from your brain.

 It means that you're accepting that

you're not going to be with that

person and accepting a new format of life.

—Sylvester McNutt III

Make a Decision

Take a physical inventory of the things that remind you of a person. If you have one thousand songs on your iTunes library and six hundred of the songs remind you of this person, then you'll never escape. Throw away the clothes they bought you or the DVDs that you guys picked out from the store. Do not be a hoarder of negativity. That is not fair to your growth. You must disconnect from the symbols that connect you back to this person. The only symbol that you'll never disconnect from is children, and that is okay. Everything else can go. Nothing in this physical world is necessary, and everything physical can be replaced with something different. I know some things hold sentimental value, but you must disconnect from useless things that hold you back from real growth. Do not feed me or yourself excuses about the sentimental value in some television set, an automobile, or even the housing complex you reside in. You can move, and you can let go of everything. We choose the attachments that we have, which means it is our choice to disconnect. If these symbols stay around, it's because we allow them to. If you want to move on from an ex, you have to be 108 percent on board with the idea. Otherwise, you're just wasting time and opportunity. So if you're in a space where you feel like you need to get over your ex, my question to you is, "How bad do you want it?"

We are rooted in nothing, and everything can change. It is a choice. If you sincerely want to move on, then you will take every single step possible to go to the next phase. Allowing your soul to stay inside of the life that is slowly killing you is literally suicide, so why kill yourself? Try something different; mix it up (if you can). I understand that this perspective comes with the expectation that you *can* switch up, but I do not see any reason why you cannot change your life. I'm not telling you to put yourself in a situation where you'd be homeless in order to get over something. However, I am telling you that I had to move across the country to get away from all the memories and thoughts of my ex-girlfriend because I couldn't do it in the environment where we dated each other. I am telling you that I changed my job, my mind-set, and my friends in order to reach a healthy state of emotional happiness.

I am telling you that I wouldn't go to events if I knew there was a chance of her being there. It took me years to get over my ex, and it was a concentrated effort, not a mistake. I wanted to love again after heartbreak, and I knew if I didn't take it seriously, I would never recover from the pain. I spoke about my first love, Xena, in my last book, *The Dear Queen Journey*. We spent our late teens and early twenties together. Those years are some of the greatest transitional periods in life, and we were lucky enough to share them with each other. Dealing with us separating was very hard for me because she was the first person who really loved me and accepted me for me. When we broke up the last time, it was her choice—over the phone as I sat in our apartment in Illinois. She was already emotionally and physically removed from the relationship. And it's those moments where you sit there with no answers, no direction, and no hope that ruin your soul. I remember sitting there on our bed in our room, and her voice came through the phone aggressive and firm. She said, "I'm done with this."

My heart fell out of its rib cage and rolled down the streets because I couldn't understand why the person who was telling me she loved me yesterday was now saying she didn't even want to speak. Once you reach a point like this, you have to remember to make a decision and then to disconnect. This applies for all phases of moving on, and not just in the dating format. I quit two corporate-America jobs in the process of becoming an international best-selling author. I literally wouldn't have been able to achieve this without sacrificing $80,000 per year to chase a dream that nobody believed in. I had to move on from the environment because it had me out of shape and overweight, and I didn't know self. You'll never elevate yourself if you allow your environment to kill your progress. Moving on is like magic because you have to believe in something that you can't even explain, but it starts with making a choice.

Closure Conversation

One of the biggest flaws that people have within their thought process around moving on, is the expectation that the person who hurt them will provide them with a valid reason as to "why" the situation needs to end. Your closure will only come when you have a realistic conversation with yourself; they don't owe you anything. Stop chasing them; they don't have the ability to help your closure process. To obtain the closure, you claim you want, you'll need to look yourself directly into the mirror and accept all of the actions and inactions that have occurred.

For every second that you allow your ex to live in

your soul, minutes of your life go by unlived,

unloved, and wasted. Let the person go like you

would a hot piece of steel burning the sensitive skin

of your precious hand if you held on to it. The

memories are normal, but the desire to try and

rekindle the flame is what's burning your happiness

now; accept that it has passed.

—Sylvester McNutt III ("No Self Harm")

Thinking of Your Ex Is Normal

This may be the most important thing you'll ever read when it comes to "How to get over an ex." That person is going to stay with you forever, because thinking of your ex is normal. A lot of people believe that getting over someone means never thinking about a person, and that is unrealistic. It is perfectly normal to think about a person who you spent a significant amount of time with. Trying to erase a memory is egregious, and you should be at peace knowing that it is normal.

If you have a dream and your ex is in the dream, it is not because you miss your ex. It is because you have a present void that he or she used to fill. In the past you loved this person emotionally and physically, and the only reason you dream of your ex is because of a missing romantic void today, and that is okay.

Getting over your ex is a process; do not think that the end goal is to never think of him or her. No, the end goal is to reach a high-level understanding of acceptance. You don't need to know why the person broke up with you, you don't need to give more effort to a dead situation, and you do not have to beat yourself up for thinking about someone, because moving on is about accepting that there is a new life waiting for you on the other side of this situation.

Dear Soul,

If your soul wants to grow and move on from anything that has caused you pain, you must accept that your ticket to success is acceptance. The longer you allow yourself to live inside of resentment, negativity, or hate, the longer you'll allow your heart to sit inside of an abyss of misery.

Acceptance is the number one most important factor in this entire process. The reason I put those steps in the start of the book is because none of this would make sense without a deep understanding of acceptance. Everything around healing and growth will forever lead us to acceptance.

Here's the thing that you must be very aware of and prepared for— there is always a test that occurs after you attempt to move on. It doesn't matter if you're moving on from an addiction, a behavior, or an ex. There is one moment that you have to be prepared for. This moment is called the "Comeback Trail," and I am about to prepare you for the Comeback.

The Comeback Trail

This part of life will literally destroy you if you are not prepared for it. By definition, the Comeback Trail is something that attempts to return to your life after you've already attempted to live without it. It's hard for me to accept a person's return after a void. I think about how I had to move on without that person. Once I do, it's just not the same. It's always interesting when people activate the Comeback Trail. I always question their motives and purpose. It just feels awkward knowing they want to come back after they've already made the decision to stay away.

In relationships, when I was younger, I was a little bit more naïve, and I tried to return to every relationship situation after we decided that it was over. This applies to relationships that weren't sexual. There were certain friendships that occurred that I returned to when I knew I shouldn't have. We all have done this. But why do we keep going back, especially when the situation has proven to be either toxic or unproductive? In my Comeback Trail theory, I want to break it down because there are a few elements that need to analysis before you risk your growth and happiness, as far as going back or accepting this old stimuli back into your new life. These pages here will show the elements to the Comeback Trail theory. The majority of the time when people leave, we need to close the door behind them. It's okay to close a door that once shed light, especially if it is nothing but darkness now.

The Approach

The first part of this theory is "the approach," and this occurs after the stimulus has been absent from your life. For example, if you've decided to stop drinking, you'll get an invite to go drink. The second you decided to move on from someone after months of trying to be with that person, and he or she wasn't having it, that individual will contact you and say, "I miss you."

Remember that these tests will approach your life and will knock you off of your center if you do not have a plan. If your plan is to move on from an ex, there is no reason to respond to this ex's messages unless you want to go back. If you're an alcoholic and you want to stop drinking, you can't even acknowledge those texts that say, *Let's meet at the bar at 7*. As people, we have to be accountable for the environments we choose to participate in. We have to understand that no matter what the situation is, the principles apply to all of them.

I need you to be mentally and emotionally prepared for the approach of the Comeback Trail because this moment will show a vivid reflection of your growth.

I wonder why souls continue to allow toxic people back into their lives once they've already realized that these creatures have a history of hurting them. It does not seem healthy to me.

Comeback Trail and Stab

Once you've been stabbed in the heart and left in the open field of nothingness, it should be easier to receive, because it can't get any worse than the bottom. Gas masks and wrist locks lie on the ground as you look around and see the torture chambers of life. Preachers yelling, "Preach," but they're blinded by their false sense of truth. You want to bounce back, and you're going to. Eventually the hellfire stops burning, the rain will evaporate, and the lonely nights will turn into nights of gold and fulfillment. You'll bounce back—and break the sound barrier when you do. Just believe in magic. Once the Comeback Trail is activated, they'll push and test your willingness to give. The persons, things, or situations that took the shine out of your sun will continue to dim your universe as long as you allow them to. Their only purpose was to shine real bright for one moment, and then they destroy you. Once you accept that their only purpose was to obliterate you, it should be easier to keep them out of your treasured life. They come around as a blessing and as something that wanted to help you. Eventually, they'll turn into the main source of your pain, yet you still stay conflicted by the dissonance in your brain. Hope is the fucking drug that you hold on to like a newborn baby as it holds his mother's index finger. Yet the pain of these occurrences hurts you deeper and deeper each time until you become numb. The initial stab is deep, cold, and usually has a twist—the initial stab is the one we never get over. So are you going to let them back in, or are you going to grow on your own?

You Need to Create Healthy Barriers

Your soul is demanding that you create barriers for yourself; it's the only way to solidify consistent health in any pillar. When we refer to the "Come Back", this is the only a factor that matters because you haven't determined what you will, and will not allow. A "healthy barrier" is an emotional understanding that of what you're willing to allow. Your emotional welfare will always be below it's potential if you allow others to dictate your input and output. The first realistic step that you can take is to turn your phone off, turn off the television and turn your soul on. The rest of your life, can be the best of your life; you must allow the universe to send you the blessings you deserve by eliminating your exposure to negativity. Look down at your palms; picture a bottle of acid being poured into them every second you allow toxic situations to linger. Your hands will not be able to handle that type of pain for long; when the acid starts to pile up, pull your hands back and say, "Enough is enough, and it's time for a change."

WE

MUST

HEAL

OUR

OURSELVES

You Are Energy

My temple is a ball of energy; moods and outcomes impact my levels. I've grown and developed from where I was years ago. I am grateful where I am today; I'm ready to keep growing. I've found a new light in being very aware of where I place my energy. I'm grateful for the lessons; excitement doesn't begin to describe my mood. The last thing I'm going to do is allow hope to kill my observation of reality. True happiness is about living in the present moment; hope kills acceptance.

HOPE: The Drug That Kills

Hope is one of the most hypnotizing, stimulating, and addictive drugs out there today in our world. I watch humans get high off of the lows of hope. This drug causes users to dive deep into emotions, when they should step back and use restraint. True power is restraint, not diving into emotions and fantasy worlds.

Why does hope stop us from moving on?

Hope stops us from moving on because we hope that the outcome will change.

Why is hope a drug, Sylvester?

In my observation of the world, anything that alters your brain from seeing clearly is a drug. Hope impairs reality all of the time, in my experience.

How do I know when to give up hope that we aren't going to get back together?

Only you have the answer to this question. I do know it is very hard to progress in team sports without the other teammates participating fully. I suppose that in my life, I demand others to be accountable for their actions. Maybe you should too, but be careful doing that, because you can only do that when you are all-in loving yourself.

How to Get

Over Trust Issues

Trust is the relationship. If there's no trust, then there is no relationship. If we have issues, we must look internally and solve them via introspection and self-awareness. Trust always starts with your view and your ability to hold yourself up when the situation wants you to drown. Do not allow insecurity, fear, or the past to block your ability to trust now. You cannot afford to waste any more time doing that. Trust is the ticket to freedom that you need.

It's beyond powerful to

let them know that you

believe in them.

It will ignite them to

the next level.

Even if that person is

you, be a believer.

Trust develops via choice and observation. Our entire population believes that trust is something that is earned over time, and I'm going to assault that logic and present you something from the mind of the Visionary Poet because when I had that mind-set, it never worked for me. My claim is that trust is a formula and that trust is a choice. In the next few pages, I will break down the elements of trust, the formula, and how to trust again. Trust is one of the most important character traits that needs to be present for self-love and self-awareness, and it should be in all healthy relationships. If you do not have trust, then you have confusion and dissonance only.

Four Elements

To Build Inner Trust

1.   Acceptance of all things

2.   Understanding of choice

3.   Knowing trust is a choice

4.   Believing forgiveness is the bridge to letting go

Acceptance of All Things

The summer came and went,
But my body was still cold from
Last winter, the winter storms destroyed
My soul and motion.
I remember resting there after I drank
Two whole bottles by myself.
She told me she was getting married and
Leaving me to pick up the broken pieces of her heart from my poor decision.
This situation made me understand karma.
My girl came in went like an earthquake.
It sliced my heart like turkey in November

I soaked.
I cried and fell to me knees.
I didn't stay there forever,
Just long enough to get my shoes dirty and to
Feel how hard the ground was.
I didn't sleep for eight days;
I was dehydrated and weak.
Another eight days and I smiled for the first time like a newborn child the first time it
experiences happiness.

Another eight days went by and I started noticing that I was happy again.
She was gone.
She was gone.
We were no more.
But after twenty-one days I was happy again.
On the twentieth night, that is when I said "fuck it" and accepted the entire situation.

Understanding of Choice

I didn't understand her choice.
I couldn't make sense of the fact that she wanted
To return me like I was a manufacturer's mistake.
My return policy wasn't set up like that.
You just can't return me when you felt like it
Without telling the manager why.

> Silly humans—we want so much control.
> How did we become so entitled?
> I should've known that I couldn't control her,
> Because she has free will.

> Never forget the other person has free will,
> And that means
> They have the choice to do what they want to.

Once I came down from my high of hope and started living at realistic lane,
I saw that she no longer wanted to park there.
It made more sense than before, and that's how I got over her. That's how I started to understand trust.

Trust is not about guessing if a person will or won't. Trust is about trusting what you see and learning from what you didn't.

If she wants to stay and love me until my dying day or if she wants to leave like the Midwest summers, either way I have no control.

> We often downplay the power of choice; you have the ability in every situation to decide your outcome. You have to break out of the prison of being a victim; be accountable, take control of your actions and responses. Most of the time, we respond emotionally and we assume. There is a lot of value in sitting back and observing without grading every situation.

—Sylvester McNutt III

Trust Is a Choice

Trust is just like the light switch
In the bedroom.

When you walk in, you have
The ability to walk around in

The dark room and hope you
Don't stub your big toe.

Or you can hit the switch
As soon as you walk in the room

And activate your eyesight.
If that light switch electrocuted you

Before, I can understand why you
Wouldn't want to put your hand

Back up here, but eventually you'll
Get tired of stubbing your toe,

Regardless of pain or past experience.
Trust is a choice.

Forgiveness Is the Bridge to Letting Go

I accepted that she was gone like 1990s.
It was a conscious choice.

The power returned to my shoulder like
An eagle as it lands on its perch.

This has been the key the whole time.
I wasn't able to trust because I was caught up

In her actions.
But I have the power because I am the one.

It felt like a lightning bolt went through my soul Once I found out that
trust is about healing and

Accepting things from your past.
After all of the pain she caused me, I was able to

forgive her.
Even if she never asked for it,

I gave it to her
Because my soul needed to heal,

And without healing
You cannot have trust.

Trust and forgiveness of the past go hand in hand.
Let Go.

Do You Feel like This?

There's no fucking way I'm going back to that lifestyle. I can't give all of myself to another person just to have everything taken and stolen like a crook.

Everything I was trying to give was taken from me like a greedy kid on Halloween who eats all of his candy in one night.

All of the people who preached love were just dirty mirrors of deceit and distaste, leaving my soul cut and broken like a dilapidated midwestern city.

No, my heart can't take any more of the lies or pain that come from people who are supposed to represent peace and love. My soul cannot bear the rotten fruit of these mongers who destroy souls and bring tears.

I'm just the ruins and mold after the hurricane came to push my soul up to the top of the atmosphere like a tornado and then allowed me to get singed like a lighting strike in Texas.

Yes, I'm struggling. My brain hurts. My soul hurts. Everything sucks because I have trust issues. I just don't know how to trust, how to love, or even where to begin with this. This generation sucks, and nobody understands loyalty. What am I supposed to do?

How to Get Over Trust Issues

Where is the lack of trust coming from? And I'm going to ask you to really dig in deep to figure out where this issue is coming from. A lot of people develop trust issues because of their own behavior. What have you done lately? Or, do you feel like some karma will come back to you from a decision you made some years ago?

You must take a full inventory of who you are and what behaviors you bring to the table, and you must have a full understanding of how your actions are impacting those around you.

Most people do not want to admit that they are the reason they do not trust people. Let me introduce the idea of fear—what is fear? According to *Wikipedia*, fear is the emotion induced by a threat perceived by living entities, which causes a change in brain and organ function and ultimately a change in behavior, such as running away, hiding, or freezing from traumatic events.

The fear component allows you to stay enslaved to your trust issues. You're jaded, and you're trapped in a minuscule mind-set that will never produce the success, love, or awareness that you claim you want, and it's your fault.

It's your fault because you haven't understood the power of fear and how deep fear goes into your day-to-day actions.

Fear is a crocodile walking through the muddy waters as you walk blindfolded down the sidewalk next to the swamp. Sooner or later this crocodile will reach out and lock its tight grip around your hip, stopping all progress, because you've refused to take off the blinders. When it comes to abolishing trust issues, you have to acknowledge the issues and then accept that you have them. For example, you check this person's phone if you feel uneasy around her or him, or you make this person walk on eggshells in order to fit your standard of living. Odds are, you currently have trust issues.

There was a time that everything was so good and wonderful, and you hold on to that moment hoping that you can force it back to be the way it was. Unfortunately, once you give more effort, that will only cause you to lose the very things you're tricking yourself into thinking you want.

When it comes to relationships, if you do not have trust, then your relationship does not exist. All you have is a conglomerate of two people who are causing hurricanes inside of each other's soul and then looking at each other perplexed, saying, "Why are we wet?"

In a relationship, if you drown a person in insecurity or self-hate, or if you allow your trust issues to control your day-to-day behavior, then your relationship will fail.

What is your intention, and

Does your behavior align

With your intention, or

Are you just living life

Without a plan and then questioning

Why there's no direction?

—Sylvester McNutt III

Say this aloud to the person

you want to fix things with,

even if that person is you.

Dear Soul,

There have been moments in my life that have caused confusion, stirred up emotion, and even pushed me right on my ass. However, I cannot and will not lie down in the victim position, because I am not a victim. I am going to be honest with myself and accept that I have been hurt, and it is *okay*. I am not going to use words that keep me trapped inside of trust issues, because I understand that with forgiveness comes growth. Growth is how I will go from the caterpillar to the butterfly that stops time as its wings flop across the skyline.

I forgive you; I forgive myself because I am a butterfly. I am accepting that trust is a choice, and I am going to actively choose to give my undivided trust again. Without trust, nothing can be sustained. I want to let go of the things that have caused me darkness, because I am the light, and I am brighter than any amount of darkness.

Trust issues cannot control me, because trust is a choice, and I am choosing to give it another go with all of my soul. I am the one. I am the most important person in my movie, and I am choosing to rewrite the script, and this is from my soul.

"Home"

Lets allow the past to
Be in the past.

I love you, today.

Lets get rid of our pride
And listen to each other's
Souls speak.
How would you feel if I was
In another person's arms?
I know how I would feel if
You were somewhere else.

We are home; lets figure
This out, please come home

Eight Steps to Overcome Trust Issues

1. **Communicate** with your partner *first* when things do not make sense. You're in a romantic relationship with that person, not your social media followers, best friends, or family.

2. **Analyze** and become aware of your behavior and your contribution to the environment.

3. If you had trust issues prior to entering the relationship, understand that your insecurity will be the death of it if you do not let go of the stimuli that caused you to be here. You cannot punish the new person for your past. I offer you **acceptance**.

4. **Say affirmations** daily around trust. Even if they're not remotely true, just say them anyway. Making a positive statement about the situation will help every day.

5. **Give trust** in situations where you gave criticism before. Give trust where you before gave doubt. Giving trust is actually crucial in the creation of trust.

6. **Trust issues are exhausting,** so don't tire yourself out trying to chase something that is not even on the same lane as your purpose. Sometimes you just have to let go of what was holding you to the trust-issue mind-set.

7. **Set a boundary** for yourself, because clearly this person hurt you before, but that doesn't mean he or she will do it again. However, it does mean you should demarcate your intentions if people continue to hurt you knowingly.

8. **Create a destination** for the relationship, because if you guys are just running around name calling, committing violations of trust, and not trying to grow as a couple, then what is the point? It will not be fun, blissful, or anything worth talking about so my challenge to you is to set a destination for where you'd like to go from a behavior standpoint. You must have this conversation with *you* first, and then your partner, subject to the situation. This should be an internal conversation that you have with yourself.

Trust Cyclone

When trust is not present between two people, they run the risk of becoming cyclones for each other's soul. Instead of causing a catastrophe inside the person you care about, the healthier option is to see when those clouds are starting to form and to build an alert system that alerts the people. The people are you and your partner. Pay attention to the climate of each island and be conscious of their interactions between each other. One may have sunshine and the other may have darkness brewing. Having a lack of trust is the easiest way to cause a natural disaster inside of your emotional health.

—Sylvester McNutt III

Trust-Issue Murder

I was uptown, the skyline draped over the murderers in my city. The main tragedy was an emotional conflict called "trust issues." This event was the death of many hearts, all relationships, and happiness. Yet the users of this drug turned into martyrs as they popped more pills of this venom. They developed deeper into hate and faced distorted demons that engulfed their prism. A lack of trust was the death of all things that they tried to brand as love. Let go, and permit the gargoyles to protect you from the demons of trust issues.

—Sylvester McNutt III

Trust Issues will kill progress
Be trust
You are trust
Trust is the oxygen to your blood
It is the water to your land
Live at trust
Inhale trust
It needs your lungs again
Trust is a choice

WE

MUST

HEAL

OUR

MEN

What Is Manhood?

Being a man is about leadership, always be accountable for your actions and learn when to enhance your abilities. Be a leader and understand when to follow. Don't allow ego to make you believe that you have all the answers; real men seek help and coaches. Manhood is about growing, developing, and not making the same mistake twice. Manhood is about agility; you have to build yourself to a point where you can always adjust and prosper. Manhood is about letting go of negativity, pettiness and the need to be correct. Some battles are not about winning or success, you have to fail in order to grow. Manhood is about knowing who you are and not being afraid to show emotion.

There isn't a realistic definition of what manhood is; you define it by your actions and sacrifices. Try to be mindful of how your actions impact others and live your life to the fullest. Manhood is an amazing journey; never compare yourself to another man. Seek to learn from other men, but there is no reason to compare your journey to his.

Four Ways to Raise Your Vibration

1. **Meditate**—There are numerous ways that you can meditate. I first found meditation through attending a local yoga class. It was a guided meditation via her teachings and soul. I recommend that everyone attend yoga and allow the teacher to guide you through a Vinyasa flow.

2. **Self-Hypnosis**—This is the ability to trick yourself. Tell yourself that you are amazing every day. Hypnosis is the ability to change your way of thinking through practice. Look in the mirror every morning and tell yourself something positive.

3. **Analyze what you subject yourself to**—What kind of music do you listen to? What movies do you watch? They play a large role in your awareness of self. Listen to cleaner music and turn off the gossip television shows.

4. **Let go of the past**—What happened to you 6.5 years ago is really irrelevant; the past is just a conceptualized idea of your imagination. Write it down, analyze it, and understand it so you can move on. The most important moment is the present moment. Do not live in the past. Learn from it, but stay away from there. Move on.

Poems From my

"Purple Cloud on Venus"

These poems were inspired by moments throughout the creative writing process of this book. That time period was February 2, 2015, until August 29, 2015. These poems did not have a place within the "flow" of the book, but they make sense for the *Dear Soul* journey. I never did extra credit in school; this is my attempt to rectify my lack of effort in school. People always ask me where I am from, and most days I feel like I am the planet Venus. These are my poems from Venus, welcome to my planet. If you follow me on social media you may have seen some of these thoughts during the year.

The Yoga Cloud

If you're lost in life, find yoga. Yoga is the connection to the divine. Yoga is your connection to mind, body and soul. It's a light, when the world is dark. Create time to meditate, and rest the brain. You deserve to breathe; you deserve an abundance of happiness. You deserve to have peace and light in your soul consistently. Remind yourself daily to let go of your judgments, your insecurities and stress. Meditate, look directly into your internal mirror and accept yourself as you are without judgment. You are the love of your life; you are the universe.

—Sylvester McNutt III

Practice Mindfulness Daily

Staying in the moment will increase happiness, reduce stress and stop excessive thinking. One of the main reasons we think "too much" is because we consciously replay stories and emotions from the past.

The problem with bringing the past up often is that it does not allow you to live in the present moment. The present moment is truly the only moment that is reality; the past does not exist and the future is just a figment of our imagination.

Mindfulness is the ability to sit in stillness without judging yourself. Every single day push yourself away from looking at things as "good" or "bad"; these are subjective and emotional viewpoints of that typically create delusions. Being mindful as a practice is about finding two to three minutes every day to sit disconnected from devices or expectation.

You can find people who can guide you through meditations for assistance. My favorite way is to play music with no words, to lie down and just allow my mind to float.

Excessive Thinking is the Root Of All Evil

"I was younger back then, more naïve. I was a victim of excessive thinking and worrying. I learned that every time I removed myself from that present moment, I created stress and anxiety. Today, I practice the art of letting things go. I don't attach my worth to physical things or to other's perception of me. I was conditioned to "react" to how others behaved. Now, I observe from a higher consciousness. There's no value in judging, excessive thinking or holding on to this pain that burns your soul. I've reached true happiness by letting go and accepting my world."

The Woman I Will Marry

I will only marry a woman that is okay with me being obsessed with her. She has to accept that she is my muse. I need a woman of passion that is okay with a man of vulnerability. I need a woman who will drop everything to catch my soul. She needs to be okay with me getting up in the middle of the night to leave her poetry in the refrigerator. She needs to be ready to receive an unlimited love; she does not deserve to be half-loved anymore. The woman I will marry is one who will acquire my passion, my soul and commitment. Love is not a game; love is life.

he Empathic Soul

Yes, I am an empath. That means that when you say you don't want me in your life, I'll try harder to stay. When you have a problem, it means we have a problem. Empathic people can feel every emotion deeper than the undiscovered truths of the ocean.

If you leave our life, we are the people who think about you everyday. We are foolish and gullible because our loyalty doesn't even exist. An empathic soul will be the most caring, loving friend you'll ever acquire. Don't manipulate or use an empathic soul; love them with every breath in your lungs.

—Sylvester McNutt III

Truth Seekers Have Less Friends

I get your disposition. You feel like I owe you an apology, but I don't see the point of doing it if it's not genuine. I don't want to be petty, but I meant what I did and what I said. I care about you, but you haven't heard the truth since your infant ears touched the oxygen in your hospital room. We need the harsh truth more than we need a pool of lies. Part of speaking the truth is accepting that everyone may not be able to sustain your pressure. I am a truth seeker and knowledge spreader, so I accept that I will not have as many friends as everyone else.

—Sylvester McNutt III

Interstellar

Writing you a poem
At four in the morning.
Imagining you looking at
The same star that my vision
Is fixated on right now.

I hope my paintbrush
Is big enough to blast your
Name across the Northern
Hemisphere
So one day we can spend
our time being lost.

Lost in the stars, found each
other through our soul
transfers, I just hope you see
your name in these stars.

Your love is interstellar.
—Sylvester McNutt III

No Walk

Walking on eggshells through this
small town because the city lights
singed the hairs off of my chest.

It was cold out here as the wind blew
And ripped a chill down my legs.

When denim hits your skin in the
winter, it
Is worse than jail.

I wanted to leave this town because
every
Where I go I recognize someone from
high school.

Every store I go to, they know my
name.
Living here is like tight roping over a
pool of
Acid.

I have to leave.

Moments

The best moments of life happen
unexpectedly.
They occur with no regard for
time or expectation.
Don't get caught up in thinking
we have the ability to capture
moments in our cell phones. No,
that is just the afterthought.
It's just a shadow of the real
presence.
Keep your eyes open—
They can find the truth.

—Sylvester McNutt III

Empathy's Light Bulb

I've been hard to reach lately. I distanced myself from the world. I've been absorbing energy from too many people, but it is not the rejuvenating kind of energy.

It is the energy where I listen and take on their problems. I look in their souls and feel their pain, and it makes my spine curve downward. I can't lift it up anymore without a spotter. I just have to fall back a little bit more until I reach a point of understanding. It's like an emotional sparring session when you listen to other people's problems, because you internalize the pain they're feeling as if you caused it. This is the life of an empathic person, but this course is nothing but destruction. The user of this behavior has to eliminate the toxic energy. If this user is you, I urge you to recognize and accept that you're not responsible for anyone's emotions other than your own. I remember my boss at my first job used to say something that has always stuck with me. She said, "Your lack of planning is not my emergency." Logically, it makes sense. Why should I break my back for you, when you haven't injured your own self for your cause? No, I'll pass because I have to take care of me, not only today but forever. Sorry if this is harsh, but my evolution has brought me here, and I am accepting that I cannot remain the way I was.

You cannot go through life taking on everyone's problems; you are a passionate soul, and you want to help people. Sometimes, you do them more harm by being their crutch; growth and maturation come from failure.

Sleeping Alone

If you're sleeping alone, don't trip too hard on your situation. Enter peace knowing that someone is praying for your soul. Your mind is going to play tricks on you and send tests your way. Try to relax the overthinking, and breathe. The answer is no, you don't actually miss your ex, you just miss what he or she used to represent. Sleep well knowing that "you are the one and that you are love." That faded memory of your ex is only a cloud of nothingness. Let it go. Breathe and relax, because you got this.

—Sylvester McNutt III

Voided Interpretations

There's a void. It's an empty shadow that is cast over my situation, and I'm not sure how to solve it.

I love my passion, and I'm obsessed with it.

It's my only purpose right now, which is purpose enough. I get frustrated sometimes because the people I go out with are just temporary because we go home to separate addresses, which is okay, but it is part of the void.

Honestly, I'm not sure if I have the ability to fall in love anymore. What is the point of giving everything to people when all they want is what they can get form you? Maybe it is a jaded mind-set, but I own it because I feel it at this present moment.

I feel like I've given all of my love away at this point.

I feel like I'm living for the pain of isolation from trusting the wrong people at the wrong time in the past.

Why can't I escape this rut? It seems like the more I think about this, the more I realize that I work way too much. It might be time to take less hours at the job and take in more time for myself.

There has to be more to this thing than just collecting direct deposits and paying bills.

I'm on a plateau.

I'm happy, but who really checks for me at night?

Who is rally there to pick me up when I get low?

I've always felt like I've been alone in life. I've fended for myself long enough, and I just want someone to fight for me like I find myself fighting to stay in this life.

The paradox is that I'm happy, but it's still not enough. I need a magic stick to help me survive a world that shuns creativity, because the only way I'll escape this mood is if I do a magic trick and make some things disappear.

Isolation is a very interesting party to attend, because it causes you to find self. It causes healing and happiness. Everything you need is already inside of you, but the other part of isolation can be loneliness and overthinking. To think excessively about anything or to process feelings of "feeling" alone often will maim and murder an attempt at happiness.

I'm on this happy plateau, but I don't want to think about being alone, because being alone is not a bad or good thing. It just is. What can be unhealthy is the attachment to the void of feeling alone. That's murder-suicide for my soul.

"Passion"

I want to be with someone who does not make me look silly for being loyal to them; I give everything I have to those people I care about. Next time, I want to be with a person who believes in the values of commitment, communication and acceptance like I do. I'm a lover full of passion; I want to give everything I have to one deserving soul.

I don't want to live
a life without love;
life without love, is
not life. It's just a
void, and love is
my purpose.

Moving on is like magic
because you have to believe
in something that you can't
even explain, but it starts
with making a choice.

"Fans"

People never miss you until they
become acquainted with your absence;
once you learn to live without them, the
void isn't that bad.

You let go, and move on; then, they try
to comeback into your life.

But, nothing stays the same.

They had a chance to love you and
didn't want it, so now they've been
promoted to fan.

They only deserve the option to watch
you be happy, elsewhere.

It is okay, not to be okay.
One day, you'll be okay, if
you're not okay today just
say, "okay". Don't beat
yourself up over anything.
You're not perfect; this is
your time to develop.

You cannot give a person blessings they are not ready for, even if that blessing is you.

10 Soul Commandments

1. Drink More Water

2. Love After Love

3. Love After Pain

4. Laugh More

5. Look Up At The Sky

6. Watch Documentaries

7. Talk Positively

8. Give 8 Hugs Per Day

9. Practice Your Creativity

10. Eat Amazing Food

January

You start to put things together;
this is when you accept that
some things are only supposed
to fall apart.

February

Hard work pays off if
you stay persistent.

The only way you'll be
successful is if you go
bat shit crazy.

Normal, does
not work.

March

People don't know what they want.

That statement is false; when they act
like they don't know what they want,
that's a red flag that means they don't
want you.

Lesson learned; actions
speak louder than shallow words.

April

Sometimes it takes time
for greatness to come into
fruition; bask in the moment.

You may return to moments
of greatness like this, but
nothing stays the same.

May

Give your best.
Don't wait for tomorrow, today
is the day to seize opportunity?

Fear will slow you down: don't
let it control you.

When it rains, it pours but that
does not mean the rain is bad.

Sometimes you need everything
to go wrong; when things start falling
apart, live in the now and allow it.

You can always rebuild after a storm.

June

Vibrate higher than
yesterday; live as if
there is no tomorrow.

Never fear giving your heart
and soul to an idea.

Every single portion of life
is nothing but an idea.

Ideas flow, and burn or
they elevate and ignite.

Allow your ideas, to be
positive and abundant.

July

If someone has passed away
this is a good moment to remember
his or her purpose; it may inspire you.

Some people are meant to show you
that you're not fully living life.

Grow, learn and risk everything
at least twice.

Death, physically or spiritually
Can give life; you have to have
Your eyes open to your blessings.

Some of them are right in front
of you.

August

This is a great moment to
look back, and appreciate everything
that has brought you to this point.

The past is nothing but a shadow
of your true identity; the future is
a twisted projection of potential.

Your path is about today; you
deserve to sit inside of each moment.

Pain knows your soul in order to
teach you the value of faith
and love.

Fly, like the birds; shake, like
earthquakes, don't give up on
the power of positive energy.

You're a being of substance and
value. Tell yourself, that you're
worthy of abundance, sustainability
and longevity.

Final Letter

If you never read another word I write, all I want you to do is believe in yourself. I want you to always work on leveling up and accepting yourself as you are. Self-mastery is about how you treat yourself; you should be taking calculated risks daily to improve your life.

Don't ever feel like you are alone. I am here with you. I just shared numerous stories of pain and progression, and to me that is life—pain and progression.

It is unrealistic to think that we have all of the answers; it's not fair to your soul to bear the weight of fake perfection. You don't need to be perfect, alone, or correct. All you have to do is strive to improve, recover, and enjoy life.

Thank you for reading this book. If you missed the first book, *The Dear Queen Journey: A Path to Self Love*, please go order it. This is the conclusion of the second book in the Dear Series, *Dear Soul*. Thank you for investing in it, and I will always be your friend.

—Sylvester

Made in the
USA
Monee, IL